From E.D. Thompson's Re

"Each week my husband and I look forward to E.D. Thompson's column in the *Westview*. E.D. brings back memories for many of us who have lived in the Nashville area for many years. We hope to be among the first to get a copy of his new book."

Fay Jennings Thompson
(No relation)
Nashville, TN

"I've enjoyed...'Nashville Nostalgia' each week since he began writing. Thanks E.D. for all the memories!"

Georgia M. DeGeorge
Pegram, TN

"I spent many years growing up in Nashville and thoroughly enjoy recalling the memories he invokes of my younger years."

Jerry Perella
Dickson, TN

"E.D.'s columns lift my vision to nobler heights to reflect on the tranquil lives of such people as Fay and Bill Thompson and Louis Nicholas. E.D. grabs us and forces us to acknowledge gratitude to teachers of the past who were good people first of all, who loved their students, and who were thoroughly knowledgeable in their fields of learning."

Carolyn Le Fay Forlines, Ph.D.
Nashville, TN

NASHVILLE NOSTALGIA

By E. D. Thompson

Westview Publishing, Inc.
Nashville, Tennessee

First Edition
Printed in the United States of America

Library of Congress Control Number: 2003115449

ISBN: 0-9744322-3-7

Cover design by Melissa Evans
   and Paula Underwood Winters
Typesetting and layout by Hugh Daniel
Image processing and other prepress work by Westview Publishing, Inc.

Published by
Westview Publishing, Inc.
P.O. Box 210183 * 8120 Sawyer Brown Rd, Suite 107
Nashville, TN 37221
(615) 646-6131
www.westviewpublishing.com

I dedicate this happy journey through Nashville Nostalgia

- to -

My deceased mother and father,
Blanche Hutton Dillingham Thompson and
Ellis Dillard Thompson, Senior
who lived in the old Nashville

- and to -

My sister,
Blanche Elva Thompson Fitzwater Griffin
who experienced many of my same memories

- and to -

My dear wife,
Sonia Anne Young Thompson
my partner in life through many Nashville nostalgic
memories

- and to -

Our two children and son-in-law,
Jeffrey Dillard Thompson
Lee Anne Thompson Parsley and
Jeffery Delton Parsley
who taught us how to appreciate the more recent Nashville

E.D. Thompson is uniquely qualified to have written this book. He was born in Nashville in 1924, and lived here for most of his life. From his memories of an older Nashville have come many interesting stories about old swimming pools, streetcars, schools, hotels, theatres, churches, sports, music, and downtown shopping on Fifth Ave.

His weekly columns in the *Westview* have stimulated a great deal of interest in how Nashville used to be. E.D. has received many letters and telephone calls from readers telling about how his column has evoked many pleasant memories for them.

E.D. and I were married in New York City on the old NBC television program called *Bride and Groom*. We are celebrating our 50th wedding anniversary on August 20, 2004. We have shared together many of these stories which you will read in *Nashville Nostalgia*.

Sonia Anne Young Thompson

Foreword

In my teaching at Tennessee State University and my announcing at radio WAMB-AM and FM, I keep the past alive and make it pertinent to the present and the future. E. D. "Buddy" Thompson's delightful book *Nashville Nostalgia*, does the same thing. Since mid-1999, my father has been regaling the readers of the *Westview* Newspaper with his warm, uplifting stories of Nashville's yesteryear. Now, many of those stories are gathered together in this book.

E. D. Thompson has lived through almost eight decades of changing Nashville life. He remembers and writes meaningfully about landmarks, churches, schools, streetcars, broadcasting, sports, food, holidays, and more. When he writes about music, he writes from the perspective of having participated in and even influenced the musical landscape of Music City USA.

Most importantly, E. D. writes in *Nashville Nostalgia* about people--local folks whom you know, you knew, or-- after having read about their fascinating lives--you wish you had known. Through it all, E. D. keeps alive the sights, sounds, aromas, tastes, history, memories, and values of this Athens of the South which we call home. Perhaps the fond remembrance of the past will enrich the future.

Things will never again be the same as they were in the Nashville of our memories and dreams, but *Nashville Nostalgia* will afford a fleeting but deeply satisfying glimpse of the past which is always out of reach but always in our hearts.

Jeff Thompson,
Tennessee State University faculty,
WAMB-AM & FM (Big Band radio) announcer,
And free-lance writer

A Tribute to the Westview Newspaper

I have had the pleasure of writing a weekly column called "Nashville Nostalgia" for the *Westview* Newspaper in Bellevue, Tennessee (a suburb of Nashville) since May 13, 1999.

Doug Underwood, the founder of the newspaper, started his career in journalism in 1949 with the *Nashville Banner*. From there he went to the *Daily Herald* in Columbia, Tennessee as a photographer, sports writer, and feature writer.

When television came to Nashville, Doug became a highly-regarded news reporter for both WSM-TV, channel 4, and WLAC-TV, channel 5.

Doug's dream was realized in 1978 when he started his own weekly, award winning newspaper in Bellevue, the *Westview*.

I did not know Doug Underwood personally, but I am well aware of the legacy he has left in the foundation of this newspaper.

It has been a pleasure to be associated with Doug's wife, Evelyn Underwood, who is the newspaper's publisher, and their daughter, Paula Underwood Winters, who is the editor.

Doug Underwood's family is carrying his dream on to mightier heights. The *Westview* Newspaper is excellent in quality, and is serving as a valuable tool in news reporting, enlightenment and entertainment to the greater Bellevue area.

E.D.T.

Nashville Nostalgia

CONTENTS

Montgomery Bell in Nashville's Past
From Meat and Potatoes to Trendy Shopping!
When Bellevue Was "Out in the Country"

Nashville's Glory Lives On - 179

West Nashville's Pride Lives On
East Nashville's Pride Lives On
North Nashville's Pride Lives On
South Nashville's Pride Lives On

Special Days of the Year - 201

NEW YEAR'S DAY
   New Years in All Generations
VALENTINE'S DAY
   Won't You Be My Valentine?
EASTER
   Happy in Your Easter Bonnet
MAY DAY
   The New Life of Spring
MOTHER'S DAY
   Let's Wish for Roses at the Steeplechase!
MEMORIAL DAY
   Honoring War's Fallen
FATHER'S DAY
   Remembering Father's Day
INDEPENDENCE DAY
   4th of July: Independence Day, and More!
SEPTEMBER 11, 2001
   Dear Joe Revisited

Introduction

After retiring from the field of education, the business world, and many years as a professional musician, E. D. "Buddy" Thompson began to write a weekly column called "Nashville Nostalgia" for the *Westview* Newspaper.

The column created a great amount of interest and excitement with the readers, as people seemed to enjoy "looking back" on the old days of Nashville and surrounding area, as well as the nostalgic spirit of the whole country.

From the many letters and telephone calls in response to this column, Thompson also receives many invitations to speak on "Nashville Nostalgia" at clubs and churches.

In the winter of 2001, Thompson was invited to teach a six-weeks class on "Nashville Nostalgia" at Vanderbilt University in their program called "Retirement Learning at Vanderbilt."

Thompson's "Nashville Nostalgia" is heard on a five-minute segment once a week on Vanderbilt's radio station, WRVU-FM 91.1, produced by Ken Berryhill.

Thompson has compiled many stories and information from his weekly columns into this book format revealing nostalgic memories of the old Nashville. His nostalgic reflections carry us even beyond the boundaries of Nashville.

Instead of just stating historical facts, Thompson has involved himself in many of the nostalgic experiences. He has written about many things in which he played a personal role.

He has been able to write about many of his personal experiences and his beloved city because he was born in Nashville in 1924, he attended Nashville public schools and George Peabody College for Teachers in Nashville. He was a Boy Scout and attended old Camp Boxwell on the Harpeth River, he served in the U. S. Army during World War II, he played professionally as a musician at radio stations WLAC and WSM when live music was used during the Golden Age of Radio, and he was a first clarinetist in the Nashville Symphony Orchestra.

Thompson played in many local dance orchestras. He played for shows coming to Nashville including Holiday on Ice, Ringling Brothers and Barnum & Bailey Circus, and performances featuring such stars as Margaret Whiting, Jimmy Wakely, Kate Smith, Engelbert Humperdinck, Sonny and Cher, Duke Ellington, Ray Stevens, Lorrie Morgan, Bobby Goldsboro, Johnny Cash, and others.

He played on radio, in television, and on recordings. He was around for much of the beginnings of Nashville's Music Row.

Thompson and his wife, Sonya, were married in New York City on the NBC television program called *Bride and Groom*.

Thompson taught music in public schools and on college faculties. He served 30 years as a church choir director, and has had two books published by CSS

Publishing Company of Lima, Ohio. *I've Heard That All My Life!* involves expressions from Scripture which are still in use today. *Fire for the Choir* involves the motivation of church choir directors and choir members.

This vast amount of experience has been assembled into a book which will hold the readers' interest, and create a nostalgic spirit which will truly make a person's life happier by remembering.

To further add to the readers' interest, Thompson has included a section titled "Times, People, Places and Things." This section gives a variety of nostalgic memories rather than centering on just one topic in looking back at the old Nashville days.

Nostalgia can bring happiness to a person's life. This book expresses the love and happiness of the old days of Nashville and beyond.

Candyland

Never Let the Child Get Away!

A wonderful story appeared in an issue of the magazine *GRIT: American Life and Traditions.* The story was titled "Mickey the Wizard." It was a story about the legendary actor, small man with a big heart, Mickey Rooney.

In this charming story, Mickey was quoted as saying, "I still have the child in me. Everybody is a child within themselves." He concluded his statement by saying, "Never let that child get away from you."

That statement said a lot to me. I think the child is still in me. I can think back on things of Nashville's by-gone days that seem very close to me, like the events happened just a short time ago.

I can grasp the same feelings and emotions as I once did as a child riding the trains with my family across the country. I can remember sitting by the coach window, listening to the "clickity-clack" of the wheels moving over the rails, watching the countryside pass, going over bridges and trestles, and reading the time table anticipating the next town or junction.

I can grasp the exciting nostalgia while thinking about going swimming at old Cascade Plunge, and eating a frozen Powerhouse candy bar from the concession stand.

I can remember the great movie theatres with their tracer lights aglow as we stood under the marquee canopy waiting to enter the show palace.

I can remember seeing the organ at the Paramount Theatre rise up to stage level at the Popeye Club on Saturday mornings. I can remember going to the stage show at the Princess Theatre on Church Street.

I remember the taste of that wonderful apple pie at Kleeman's on Sixth Avenue, and those great treats at Candyland at Seventh and Church. I can remember eating at Shacklett's Cafeteria.

I can remember shopping at Loveman's, Harvey's, Castner-Knott, and Cain-Sloan companies.

I can remember climbing the steps up to the top of the old Dutch windmill in Shelby Park.

I can remember watching the baseball games at Centennial Park, and buying a snow cone at the large concession stand across the street from the outdoor bandstand in the park.

I can remember going swimming at old Willow Plunge in Franklin, diving into that refreshing water, having a picnic lunch out on the sloping, green grass, and listening to the tunes of the day coming out of the loud speakers played by the big, name bands of the day.

I can remember going to the wrestling matches at the old Hippodrome. Some fine acts were brought in by Nick Gulas.

I can remember walking up the glorious staircase in the old Maxwell House Hotel, and realizing that I was walking in the steps of generals and presidents.

I can remember riding the streetcar home from Hume-Fogg High School each day. Only once did the streetcar come a little early, and I had to dash out of the school's side door onto Eighth Avenue, and dive in the back window of the Belmont Heights streetcar before I got left.

I remember going to Sulphur Dell to see the Nashville Vols play the Memphis Chicks, the Atlanta Crackers, the Birmingham Barons, or some other Southern Association team. I could watch the Vol's Larry Gilbert manage and give signals to the team, I could enjoy hearing Steamboat Johnson call the game from behind the plate, and watch Johnny Mahalic play second bass and Buster Boguskie play short stop.

As a youngster, I remember listening to the radio dramas, getting my homework, and playing with the other kids out under the streetlight.

I can remember, as if it were yesterday, going to the Tennessee State Fair, looking around the Woman's Building with my family, and carrying away our gifts of a yard stick, paint stirrer, a card of sewing needles, and maybe some pencils.

I remember wearing a red flower to church on Mother's Day.

I remember when my sister and I would fly out of the door into the cold, wintry air on Christmas morning to see what all of our friends had gotten.

I can still grasp the excitement through my nostalgic spirit of going downtown to Fifth Avenue, shopping amidst the crowd in the Five & Ten Cent stores, smelling those roasted peanuts and hot cashews; but, mainly I can remember greeting my friends and looking in their sacks with great excitement to see what they had bought.

Yes, let's not allow the child to get away from us. Let's stay in good health, with alert minds and bodies, and think like a child, remembering the positive happenings and the outpouring of happiness in our lives.

Sometimes when I speak about "Nashville Nostalgia" at various churches, clubs, and other places, a tear might come to my eye. And, yes, children cry, too. So, it is O. K. if sometimes we even cry.

Let's never let the child get away from us.

Retirement Learning at Vanderbilt

I was invited to teach a six-weeks course on "Nashville Nostalgia" at Vanderbilt University in the Winter of 2001. This university program, in which many subjects are taught to senior citizens throughout the year, is called "Retirement Learning at Vanderbilt."

The class and I had a wonderful time. You can imagine when seventy-five to one hundred citizens get together, there is a lot to talk about. Also, I was surprised that such a large number of these class members were born in Nashville as I was.

I gave each member of the class a copy of the *Westview* containing my "Nashville Nostalgia" column. Some of the people were *Westview* readers.

Each of the six class sessions was exciting, and each presented something new. Following the class session in which we talked about our "Blizzard of '51," a gentleman brought in an old Chattanooga newspaper which had many wonderful pictures of their ice storm in 1960. His pictures were about equal to our ice storm pictures some nine years before.

When I mentioned that the end of the streetcar line for the old Belmont Heights streetcars was on Belmont Boulevard at Cedar Lane, a class member brought up about us kids coming down Cedar Lane hill on sleds. He asked, "Wasn't there a fatality there?" We kids used to go to the top of Cedar Lane hill, and build a bon fire to stay warm in the wintry weather. Also, we would post a group of friends down at Belmont Boulevard to stop the cars when someone was coming down the steep hill on a sled.

I told this class member that there was never a fatality to my knowledge. But, a high school student by the name of Rip Blackmer came down the hill, lost control, and crashed into the stone wall at the bottom of Cedar Lane hill at Belmont Boulevard. Rip was not killed, but his arm became paralyzed. That taught all of us a lesson.

One person in the class asked about the old home in Sevier Park on Granny White Pike. Many years ago, I and the kids in my neighborhood used to pass that old house many times as we headed out to Brown's Creek or to walk the old Glendale streetcar tracks which were where Lealand Lane now stands. We had no idea of the great history surrounding that old house in Sevier Park.

We uncovered the facts that the old house is called Sunnyside Mansion. Before the Civil War, the mansion served as the home of Mrs. Jesse Benton, sister-in-law of statesman and artist Thomas Hart Benton. She was the widow of Jesse Benton who left Nashville after a feud with Andrew Jackson.

Sunnyside was built in the mid-1800s, and it was purchased and restored in the 1920s by Colonel Granville Sevier who was a foster grandson of the Bentons.

What is more interesting is that this site is reputed to have been a trading post with the Chickasaw and Choctaw

Native-Americans. Timothy Demonbruen was said to have done fur trading there.

Metro Parks Department bought Sunnyside Mansion in 1945 from the estate of Colonel Sevier. Sunnyside Mansion still bears scars from the Battle of Nashville.

At one class session, we talked about Hillsboro High School burning in 1952. I was the band director at Hillsboro High from 1948 until 1954. I found out that four people in the class were at Hillsboro as students. One of them, Wallace Edwards, played clarinet in the band which I directed. I had not seen Wallace for almost 50 years.

During class, I made the statement that I owned all of the Hillsboro annuals during the years I taught there except one. It was the 1952-53 annual covering the fire. The next class session, Wallace brought me a copy of that annual as a gift. What a treasure.

Two other exciting things happened during our class time while enjoying "Nashville Nostalgia." We learned that two class members were relatives of people whom we discussed in class.

We discussed Lucinda "Granny" White who operated an Inn on the south side of Nashville during the 1800s. When travelers from the south arrived at Granny White's Inn, which was noted for its cleanliness and good food, they knew that they were close to Nashville.

Granny White's grave is located off Granny White Pike a short distance in from Otter Creek Road. A subdivision is built there now called Granny White Inns. Her grave is preserved and sits 200 feet from where her old Nashville Inn was located.

We learned that a class member, Mr. Walter Hardcastle, was a distant relative of Granny White. He knows many facts. He owns a copy of her will. And, thanks to Mr. Hardcastle, I too now own a copy of Granny White's will. That brings nostalgia right inside the classroom.

Then, there was a class session when we talked about old Hume-Fogg High School. I explained that Alfred Hume was the first superintendent of schools in Nashville, and Francis Fogg was the first president of the Board of Education. The school which still exists at Eighth Avenue and Broad Street was named Hume-Fogg in honor of those two gentlemen.

At this moment, a lovely lady seated on the third row stood up and said that she was the great-great-granddaughter of William Hume. I immediately said, "Do you mean the Reverend William Hume who was the father of Alfred Hume for whom the school was named?" She said, "Yes."

This brought our topic of discussion to a much higher level to be honored by the presence of Harriet Jones Doermann. Of course, immediately someone took her picture. What a thrill to have a class discussion move into such a high-level direction with such a high-level of intensity!

Thanks to Marion Couch who invited me to teach the classes, and thanks to Silvine Hudson for her efficient direction of Retirement Learning at Vanderbilt.

———

During the class sessions, I refrained from offering too much information about our Nashville beginnings. I felt that it may not hold the same nostalgic interest by discussing historical facts before our time.

I was wrong! At about the fourth class session, I began to bring out some historical facts about the Old Nashville, and saw the reaction.

Following each one-hour-and-fifteen-minute-class session of the six-weeks course, many class members usually came up and made a circle around me to continue the joyful discussion of the day, and show their enthusiastic interest. After the class in which I brought out some historical facts, one man said, "Today has been the best session of all!"

So, I guess the readers of this book should have the opportunity to delve into a little of the Old Nashville history, also.

Fisk Jubilee Hall

Old City Cemetery

A Little History
of the Old Nashville

Many things did happen before any of us came along.

Courthouse on Public Square, c. 1920s

Nashborough on the Cumberland Bluffs

I have never referred to my newspaper columns as being history. Instead, I want to reveal a nostalgia, a feeling, and a spirit of the old days in Nashville. However, the column is about Nashville's past, so I guess that does make it history.

Since that has been said, I realize that all Nashvillians and others should be interested in some older history about our great city before our time of living here.

The city of Nashville was founded by real frontiersmen and women who moved west over many obstacles of nature to arrive on the rich banks of the Cumberland River. They moved to new land called French Lick.

Archaeological evidence tells us that Native-Americans of Mississippian culture and others lived in the area from 1000 to 1400 A. D. We are told that they raised corn, made earthen mounds, and painted beautiful pottery.

The Cherokees, Chickasaws and Shawnees later used the area as a hunting ground.

The French were the first white people to establish a nucleus of commerce here in the early 1700s. Around 1765, a French-Canadian trader by the name of Timothy Demonbreun settled near the Salt Lick. He later became an important political figure in the history of Nashville. [For you French students, his correct name was Jacques-Timothe De Montbrun.]

There is a curious old cave up above the Cumberland River within the bluff on the west bank where Timothy Demonbreun first lived. It can easily be seen from a boat on the river.

Demonbreun died here in 1826, and is buried in the Old City Cemetery on Fourth Avenue, South.

We still have a major downtown street named Demonbreun Street which has developed over the many years. Today it is close to our modern arena, new Country Music Hall of Fame, and the new Hilton Suites Nashville hotel. What changes this area of Nashville has seen since the days of Timothy Demonbreun!

Tennessee was first a portion of North Carolina. In 1778, James Robertson scouted our Nashville area with eight other men. The next year, Robertson returned with approximately 250 people to build a permanent settlement.

Also, a partner of James Robertson named Colonel John Donelson brought some families over 1,000 miles by boat down the Holston, Tennessee, Ohio, and Cumberland rivers arriving in April of 1780 to these Cumberland Bluffs.

The Cumberland Compact, which was the first civil government in Middle Tennessee, was signed by 256 men. They named the settlement Nashborough for General Francis Nash of North Carolina who was a hero in the Revolutionary War. The name later was changed to Nashville. Today, we can enjoy the replica of the old Fort Nashborough located on First Avenue, North just above Broad Street and the Hard Rock Café.

In 1796, Tennessee had become the sixteenth state in our United States. Nashville benefited by being on the banks of the Cumberland, and the settlement began to grow. Steamboats traded with cities such as Pittsburgh and New Orleans. Banking, printing, and publishing industries began to appear in Nashville.

Also, Nashville began to experience a strong political influence at the time when Andrew Jackson began to attract national attention. In 1828, General Andrew Jackson became the first "western president" of the United States.

After two terms as president, Andrew "Old Hickory" Jackson retired to his home, The Hermitage, near Nashville. He is buried on the grounds of The Hermitage beside his beloved wife, Rachel, daughter of John Donelson.

Many early settlers, including Nashville's founder, James Robertson, are buried in the Old City Cemetery on Fourth Avenue, South.

It is interesting to note that our Charlotte Avenue is named for Charlotte Robertson, the wife of James Robertson. Nashville still endears itself with many names of the Old Nashville.

For instance, we have surrounding communities with the names Donelson, Hermitage, and Old Hickory. In addition to Charlotte Pike and Demonbreun Street named for people in Nashville's history, I can think of the James Robertson Parkway below the capitol building, the Andrew Jackson Parkway, Old Hickory Boulevard, McGavock Pike for the McGavocks dating back to the late 1700s, Harding Road named for the owner of the Belle Meade Plantation, Acklen Avenue for Joseph and Adelicia Acklen, Deaderick Street named for George Deaderick, Nashville's first banker, and many others.

We have the Ryman Auditorium named for old steamboat captain, Thomas Ryman. Overton High School is named for John Overton, a great friend of Andrew Jackson, who came to Nashville shortly before Tennessee became a state. Overton became a judge in the state Supreme Court.

Other schools bear such names as Davidson Academy, McGavock High School, Robertson Academy, Donelson Christian Academy, Harding Academy, Montgomery Bell Academy, Hume-Fogg High School, named for educators Alfred Hume and Francis Fogg. After the death of Hume, Joshua F. Pearl was named superintendent of Nashville's public schools. For many years, we had a Pearl High School. Today, we have a school with the name Pearl-Cohn.

State office buildings downtown are called the Andrew Jackson Building, Rachel Jackson Building, and James K. Polk Building. The Cordell Hull Building is named for a past Secretary of State from Tennessee who served in the cabinet of President Franklin D. Roosevelt.

The three performance halls in the Tennessee Performing Arts Center are named Andrew Jackson Hall, James K. Polk Hall, and Andrew Johnson Hall for the three United States presidents from Tennessee.

This is just a thimble full of Old Nashville names and Old Nashville history, but it is enjoyable to see just how close we still live to the names and places from our old Nashborough on the Cumberland Bluffs.

Jubilee and Old Glory Still Fly

I was born in Nashville, and I always knew of the existence of the Old City Cemetery at the corner of Fourth Avenue, South and Oak Street in South Nashville. However, my knowledge of the more intimate facts about the historic value of the cemetery mounted greatly during the 1950s. This is when my wife's father took over some responsibility for the Nashville historic landmark.

My father-in-law, Mr. T. C. Young, was in the coal business for many years. He was an active member in the Methodist Church. He was instrumental in the founding of the Nashville Layman's Club. He served on the Nashville City School Board for many years.

After Mr. Young retired from the coal business, he was asked by Mayor Ben West to oversee the working of the Old City Cemetery.

It was not like Mr. Young to just sit, see that the grass was cut, and have a grave opened when needed. He decided to do research and work with some historians in Nashville to bring the old cemetery to the forefront of Nashvillians' education and pride.

The cemetery was Nashville's first public cemetery which opened in 1822, and has become a wonderful tour for adults, tourists, and a historical field trip for Nashville area school children. There are many interesting things one can learn by a visit to the Old City Cemetery.

Among those buried there is General James Robertson (1742-1814) who is considered to be the founder of Nashville. Robertson died near Memphis and was buried there, but re-interred in our Old City Cemetery in 1825.

General Robertson's wife, Charlotte Robertson, also is buried in the old cemetery as well as their son, Dr. Felix Robertson, who was the first white child born in Nashville. Felix was twice mayor of Nashville, and a professor of medicine at the old University of Nashville.

Also buried in the cemetery is Anne Robertson Cockrill who was the sister of General Robertson. Anne was a teacher and the mother of Mark Cockrill who won world renown as a breeder of fine sheep.

Buried there also is Alfred Hume, who along with a lawyer by the name of Francis B. Fogg, are considered to be the fathers of Nashville's public school system.

In the cemetery you can see the graves of Mabel Lewis Imes and Ella Sheppard who were members of the original Fisk Jubilee Singers.

The fine singing group, the Fisk Jubilee Singers, was formed to serve as a public relations and money raising entity to save and support the university during its financial difficulties. The Jubilee Singers went on tour in 1871 to raise money which took them to the North, East, the White House in Washington, and even to Europe. That tour raised enough money to get the university out of debt, buy land for the campus, and build Jubilee Hall which is still there today. The Fisk Jubilee Singers still exist on campus.

Another big attraction in the Old City Cemetery is the grave of Captain William Driver (1803-1886.) He was the person who gave the American flag the name "Old Glory."

William Driver was an old sea captain. He flew his country's flag from the mast of his first vessel on a voyage to the South Pacific. Driver moved from Massachusetts to Nashville in 1837. Two of his brothers lived here. Captain Driver became a member of Christ Episcopal Church which is now named Christ Church Cathedral located at the corner of Ninth Avenue and Broadway.

Mr. T. C. Young played a role in getting permission to fly the American flag over Driver's grave twenty-four hours a day. At that time, the only other person to whom this honor was granted was Francis Scott Key who wrote the words to "The Star Spangled Banner," our National Anthem.

Of the many other notable people buried in the Old City Cemetery, are Timothy Demonbreun, Senator Felix Grundy, Governor William Carroll, General Felix Zollicoffer, Mr. And Mrs. Henry M. Rutledge whose fathers signed the Declaration of Independence, and 14 mayors of Nashville, among many others.

A trip to the Old City Cemetery would be valuable for everyone. A city's population needs to have a knowledge and understanding of its history so that the city has a foundation of values to offer its citizens.

How Close Are We to the Declaration of Independence?

I enjoy visiting Rutledge Hill just south of downtown Nashville. It is nice to stand on the hill and behold a panoramic view of that area of the city, framed by the skyline of downtown Nashville.

Rutledge Hill is located near the Children's Theatre building and the old Howard School building which is now occupied by Metro government offices. You can drive around Second Avenue South, and First Avenue South in the vicinity of such streets as Rutledge Avenue, Middleton Street, Lea Avenue, and Peabody Street and be in historic Rutledge Hill.

A few years back, developers began to clean up, remodel, renovate, and give life to this area of Nashville overlooking the Cumberland River and downtown Nashville. Many citizens began to purchase homes and apartments in the once elite area which once again is becoming elite.

Back in the 1800s, many prominent people lived on Rutledge Hill. Named after the Rutledge family, the Hill still has several old structures which we can enjoy today.

Henry M. Rutledge was married to Septima Sexta Middleton. Both of their fathers had signed the Declaration of Independence. Septima Sexta was Mrs. Rutledge's name, and in Latin her name means Seventy-six as in 1776.

Also, it should be noted that during early Nashville times, a lawyer by the name of Francis B. Fogg helped to found Nashville's public school system, and he was married to Mary Middleton Rutledge. Mary was the granddaughter of Rutledge and Middleton, both of whom had signed the Declaration of Independence.

If you are interested in sight seeing, you can visit the site of Thomas Green Ryman's old home on Rutledge Hill. Ryman was the steamboat captain who built the Union Gospel Tabernacle on Summer Street (Fifth Avenue, North). Later, upon the death of Thomas Ryman, the structure was renamed Ryman Auditorium.

Ryman's home was on Second Avenue, South (then known as South Market Street) near Lea Avenue. You can still see the concrete gate posts where his home stood. The large Queen Anne frame house with a slant roof, seven gables, and two turrets, served as home for Captain and Mrs. Ryman and their seven children from 1885 until 1926.

I am sure many of you have seen his home. It wasn't torn down until 1940.

On Rutledge Hill today, the city has reserved a nice, grassy park area to be enjoyed by us citizens--citizens not too far removed from the children of the signers of the Declaration of Independence.

Captain Tom Built It as a Church

Captain Thomas Green Ryman, who owned thirty-five steamboats on the Cumberland River, dropped in on a tent meeting held by the evangelist, Sam P. Jones. This experience transformed Ryman's life. Captain Ryman converted to the Christian gospel, and spent a lot of money to promote temperance and Christian evangelism.

Captain Ryman built the Union Gospel Tabernacle on Summer Street (which today is called Fifth Avenue, North) where Sam Jones and other evangelists could hold revivals.

When riverboat Captain Tom Ryman died in 1904, Sam Jones preached his funeral in the Tabernacle to a packed house. It was then that Jones suggested that the name of the building be changed to the Ryman Auditorium.

Over a period of time, the religious purposes to which the auditorium had been built began to expand and serve as an entertainment and lecture forum.

As small as Nashville was back in those times, there was an enormous array of celebrities who performed at the Ryman Auditorium. The Ryman stage saw such actors as Will Rogers, Sarah Bernhardt, Helen Hayes, Katharine Hepburn, Basil Rathbone, Orson Welles, Bela Lugosi, Ethel Barrymore, Harry Houdini, Charlie Chaplin, and Bob

Hope. Singers such as Helen Traubel, Nelson Eddy, Jeanette MacDonald, Enrico Caruso, Lily Pons, and Marian Anderson brought their musical talents to Nashville.

Radio station WSM leased and operated the Ryman Auditorium from 1941 until 1963 when the house was given the name "Grand Ole Opry House."

But, I want to tell you why I have such wonderful memories of the Ryman Auditorium. I remember the dear and gracious Lula C. Naff who booked engagements and was the efficient manager of the Ryman for fifty years. She collected posters of the stars who performed at the Ryman. Many of the museum pieces you can see now in the glass cases at the rear of the auditorium are from her collection.

I was a good friend of Harry Draper who did a wonderful job as manager of the Ryman after the death of Lula Naff. Harry was a violist who played in the staff orchestra at WSM radio in the 1940s, and in the Nashville Symphony Orchestra.

I remember sitting on the stage of that great old auditorium back in the 1940s as a musician in the Nashville Symphony. We played many rehearsals and concerts there with some marvelous, nationally known artists as the soloists.

The auditorium has tremendous acoustics. The sound is so remarkable that many recordings, radio, and television shows have originated from the Ryman Auditorium.

I especially remember a Saturday afternoon in 1949 when our symphony played an hour program over the NBC radio network. The hour long NBC radio program was called "Orchestras of the Nation." On that particular show, conductor William Strickland and the Nashville Symphony Orchestra were featured, and the NBC network carried the concert live across the nation. The announcer was WSM's David Cobb.

Also, I remember playing the Ryman when the Broadway musical *Oklahoma* came to Nashville for some performances. Later, Sonia, my wife, told me that she was in the audience for a performance. We didn't know each other at the time.

Later, in March 1949, Sonia and I both performed *A German Requiem* by Brahms at the Ryman. I played in the symphony, and Sonia sang in the Nashville Choral Society.

The newspaper man, Ed Sullivan, had a wonderful variety show on early television. TV had not been in Nashville very long when we enjoyed his program. His well-liked TV show was first called *Toast of the Town*. The show later took on the name *The Ed Sullivan Show*. It was a variety show with many famous entertainers. TV was in black and white back then.

In the early 1950s, when I was the band director at Hillsboro High School, Ed Sullivan came to town to be the master-of-ceremonies for a big, local variety show at the Ryman. The Hillsboro Band was asked to play a short concert at the beginning of the show. It was a thrill for my students to perform on the same Ryman Auditorium stage with the famous Ed Sullivan.

In the early 1970s, I got to play on one of Johnny Cash's television shows at the Ryman over the ABC television network. Bill Walker was the orchestra leader, and Johnny's guest star for that particular show was Bob Dylan.

We should be thankful that the prodigious, old auditorium still stands and is still in use. Once a visitor asked me why the seats were like church pews. I had to answer him by saying, "When Captain Tom Ryman built it, it was a church!"

Today, most people go in and sit on one of those old church pews to see a show. When I walk into the Ryman, my memories are flooded with the great magic of radio and television in which I played a small part.

Nashville's Higher Education Began Early

We Nashvillians today are able to walk on the old campus and in an old building which dates back to the beginning of George Peabody College for Teachers. I, among many other Nashvillians, can be carried back in history as we move from the old area near Rutledge Hill to the present college campus on Twenty-first Avenue, South from where many of us graduated.

Let's go back to the founding father of our Nashville. Nashville was five years old when James Robertson traveled to Raleigh and there convinced the legislature of North Carolina (of which Tennessee was then a part) to grant a charter for the founding of an academy available to the youth of Nashville.

Upon Robertson's return, Davidson Academy was established. Dr. Thomas B. Craighead was elected president and main teacher of the Academy. The Academy was located about six miles to the north of Nashville.

Soon, it was felt that the school should be closer to the population and have a more pretentious name. So, in 1806, the school was re-chartered as Cumberland College, and moved into town near the area which we now call Rutledge Hill, south of downtown Nashville.

The school had problems, but Nashvillian Felix Grundy played a great role in keeping the school in operation.

In 1824, Dr. Philip Lindsley was chosen to lead the college, which now had been renamed the University of Nashville. The name Cumberland was not used because the new Cumberland Presbyterian Church denomination had just organized a Cumberland College at Princeton, Kentucky. (By the way, when that college ran into difficulties, it was moved to Lebanon, Tennessee where it is still located today as Cumberland University.)

The University of Nashville was an institution of very high standards and demanded excellence in academics. There were graduated such historic family names in Nashville as Fosters, Ewings, Nichols, McGavocks, Donelsons, Hayes, Hardings, Goodletts, Overtons, and Craigheads.

When Philip Lindsley resigned as president, his son, John Berrien Lindsley, became president. His views were on expansion. The school opened a medical department. President Lindsley opened a military department. He opened a preparatory department made possible by a bequest from Mr. Bell, this area's iron manufacturer, which we still know today as Montgomery Bell Academy.

The university was always accustomed to lean years, but finances were becoming even worse.

In 1867, after the Civil War, George Peabody of Massachusetts gave two million dollars for the help of "our stricken, sister Southern states" in the development of teachers.

After years of negotiations, the money was applied to the University of Nashville to promote the education of teachers. Thus began the State Normal College, known after 1889 as the Peabody Normal College, and after 1906 as George Peabody College for Teachers.

Later, the decision was made to move the college from the campus near Rutledge Hill to the Hillsboro section of town near Vanderbilt University. In 1914, Peabody College opened on Twenty-first Avenue, South with Dr. Bruce Ryburn Payne as its president.

Upon Bruce Payne's death in 1937, Professor S. C. Garrison of the department of psychology succeeded him. In January 1945, he too died suddenly. Dr. J. E. Brewton served during the following interval.

Then, in September, Dr. Henry H. Hill became the president of Peabody College and was president when I was a student there. Other presidents have followed Dr. Hill.

A final decision was made in 1979 for Peabody College to merge with Vanderbilt University and became one. Today, George Peabody College of Vanderbilt University serves as the college of education at Vanderbilt.

If you are interested in walking on the floors, and touch and see the same things that the old, pioneer educators of the University of Nashville touched and saw, then you might want to walk in that old building off of Second Avenue, South which is between Lindsley Avenue and Middleton Street. For a time, that old building was the Nashville's Children's Museum, and on the north end of it is still the Children's Theatre. That old, fort-like building today houses the present Metro Planning Commission.

The building is more than 150 years old. It has endured the stress of war, and the wear of time. The building was well-built.

It was the main building of the University of Nashville from 1852 until 1862. The Western Military Institute was housed in this building. The building was used as a war hospital by the Union forces for a time. For 12 years, Vanderbilt University's classes in medicine were taught in that building.

In 1875, it became the main building of the beginnings of Peabody College, and continued until 1911 at which time Peabody began building its present campus on Twenty-first Avenue, South.

Finally, the state of Tennessee came into possession of the old building.

Fate would not allow the old building to be destroyed. During the administration of Governor Gordon Browning, the old, fort-like building was made available for the Children's Museum, and the building still stands today.

From Front Street to Spruce Street

In case you have forgotten, let's think about the old names of the downtown Nashville streets.

Beginning down at the Cumberland River, First Avenue used to be called Front Street. Also, when I was a child, we referred to the area of Front and Broad Streets next to the river as the Wharf. On Sundays we would ride by there, open the car windows, and hear the sidewalk preachers on the Wharf.

Second Avenue was Market Street. It was the area of warehouses and old companies designed for loading and unloading merchandise. I guess the right name was given to Market Street. Back in the old days, I am sure no one thought about renovating some of the areas for apartment living as we have today, much less the present tourist development on old Market Street.

Third Avenue was called College Street. I presume the street was named College Street because going south on that street from Broad Street would take you out to the old institution of higher learning which survived an evolution of names, eventually becoming George Peabody College for Teachers.

Fourth Avenue was called Cherry Street. I remember that mainly because that was the street on which was located the famous old Maxwell House Hotel.

Fifth Avenue was Summer Street, which became the downtown mecca of the shopping area. This used to be the crowded shopping area of ladies' and mens' wear, Five & Ten Cent stores, shoe stores, dress shops, hat shops, and the meeting ground for happy Nashvillians.

Sixth Avenue was called High Street. During my childhood, on the corner of Sixth and Church Streets was a twelve-story building. I first remember it as the Warner Building. Then, it was named the Sudekum Building. Finally, before its razing, it was called the Tennessee Building. Now, the corner of Sixth and Church is occupied by the modern high-rise Cumberland Apartments.

Seventh Avenue was called Vine Street. The Vine Street Christian Church and the Vine Street Temple moved from there some years ago to their present locations on West End or the Harding Road area.

Eighth Avenue, onto which the streetcar tracks turned off of Church Street, was called Spruce Street. I remember that Sears and Roebuck used to be in the building at the corner of Eighth and Church Streets. The Tulane Hotel was located across the street from the Sear's location.

The streetcar tracks "moved" on down Eighth Avenue to the corner of Broad Street where Hume-Fogg High School still stands. The streetcar tracks on which I rode the Belmont Heights car turned right at Broad and headed on out west.

When I was a child, I recall my father referring to First Avenue as Front Street. Also, I remember him referring to Eighth Avenue as Spruce Street.

Only in recent years, have I stopped referring to Charlotte Avenue downtown in front of the state capitol as Cedar Street.

Fifth Avenue (old Summer St.) between Church & Union Streets

Nashville Has Its Share of Mansions

Most citizens who live in various cities around the country seldom take advantage of the sights of the city in which they live, but tourists will. How many of you Nashvillians have been to the *Grand Ole Opry*? How many of you have walked around Radnor Lake? How many of you have walked around the remains of Fort Negley? How many of you have been to the 30th floor of the L & C Tower? How many of you have been inside Traveller's Rest?

Probably many Nashvillians have never taken the time to experience some of the fine mansions in our city.

Belle Meade Mansion is one of the grand plantation mansions of Old Nashville. The land, originally known as Dunham's Station, was purchased by John Harding around 1807. The original home was damaged by fire, but in 1853, the home was rebuilt and enlarged, and remains today much as it was prior to the Civil War. A portion of the Battle of Nashville was fought on the front lawn of the mansion.

Belle Meade was developed into a leading thoroughbred stud farm by William Giles Harding. Belle Meade was the home of the 1881 English Derby winner, Iroquois, the first American-born horse to win that famous race.

The Belle Meade plantation covered a vast area in the old days. There was a race track for training horses located approximately where the Belle Meade United Methodist Church sits today.

General William Giles Harding gave 2,600 acres of land to his daughter, Mary Elizabeth Harding. That same year, Mary and her husband, United States senator Howell E. Jackson, bought another 131 acres of land adjoining the larger acreage. In later years, their land became what is now our residential area called West Meade.

That beautiful family home called **West Meade** is still located at the corner of Highway 70 and Old Harding Pike beside Vossland Drive. The recent people that bought the home have made it and the landscaping very attractive.

During the Civil War, the **Belmont Mansion** survived and stands today as a reminder of Nashville's days gone by. It was built between 1849 and 1853. It was the summer home of Joseph and Adelicia Acklen. It is located at the front setting of Belmont University on Wedgewood Avenue. On the grounds, a 105-feet brick water tower was erected to provide irrigation for the beautiful gardens on the property.

Adelicia Acklen was a Nashvillian by birth. The wealthy Adelicia made Belmont the social center of Nashville, the state of Tennessee, and much of the South.

Cheekwood is Nashville's home of the beautiful Tennessee Botanical Gardens and a home for the Museum of Art. The mansion was built in 1932 during The Great Depression by Mr. And Mrs. Leslie Cheek of the Cheek family Maxwell House Coffee fame. The name Cheek was from Leslie, and the wife of Leslie Cheek was named Wood. Thus, the name **Cheekwood**.

The three-story stone Georgian mansion sits on a hilltop overlooking 55 acres of gardens, greenhouses, and magnificent Tennessee surroundings.

The **Hermitage** was the home of Andrew Jackson, the seventh president of the United States. Following a fire, the mansion was rebuilt in 1834. A visit to the Hermitage takes you back to sights prior to the Civil War. On the grounds are the tombs of Rachel and Andrew Jackson.

Close by is **Tulip Grove**. Back in 1836, it was the home of Andrew Jackson Donelson who was Rachel Jackson's nephew. He served as President Jackson's secretary in Washington, D. C.

The location takes its name from our state tree which is the tulip poplar. A stand of tulip poplars existed here near The Hermitage. President Martin Van Buren is credited with suggesting the Tulip Grove name during a visit with Andrew Jackson.

Traveller's Rest located off of Franklin Road also takes us back in history. It was the home of John Overton. He was instrumental in developing the political career of Andrew Jackson. Overton was also a lawyer and a Tennessee Supreme Court judge.

Back in those old days, homes were built in sections. The first section of Overton's home was built in 1799. The first expansion was in 1808. The house was completed in 1828. Some of the original furniture pieces are still there in the home.

Overton's mansion, property, and wealth passed on to his son, John Overton, Jr. who was referred to as "The Colonel." He continued his father's financial success. The Colonel finished building the old Maxwell House Hotel at the corner of Cherry Street (now Fourth Avenue, North) and Church Street.

I was glad to see that **Rock Castle** was decorated for a colonial Christmas on a past December, and was open to the public appearing much as when General Daniel Smith and his family celebrated the holidays there in the late 18th and early 19th centuries. The surveys of Daniel Smith were the basis for most of the early maps of Tennessee. Smith was in the party of surveyors that fixed the boundary between Kentucky and Tennessee.

If you haven't been inside the **Tennessee Governor's Mansion** located on South Curtiswood Lane off of Franklin Road, then you have missed one of the nicest. I remember the previous governor's mansion on West End Avenue. It was a sad day when that mansion was torn down and a fast food restaurant was built at that location. Now, even that fast food restaurant is gone.

The present Tennessee's executive residence was originally called **Far Hills** because of the beautiful view. The home was built for the William Ridley Wills family in 1929.

The Gregorian Colonial brick home is set on ten acres, and includes a reflecting pool, swimming pool and pool house, tennis court, putting green, greenhouse, vegetable garden, guest house and garages. The mansion has 16 rooms and 9 baths.

If you have ever seen a picture of 19th century downtown Nashville, there were no skyscrapers, but many townhouses were spread over the area. Did you know that there is still one of those 19th century townhouses standing today on Eighth Avenue, North?

We cannot really call this townhouse a mansion, but it is a significant structure due to its age and history. At 167

Eighth Avenue, North, we can see the **Savage House**. Today, this is a Bed and Breakfast location. Attached is the Towne House Tea Room. The old wooden porch and wooden front doors show their age with great character.

This location was Lot 163 of the original plan of Nashville. The property passed through ownership by John Overton in the 1700s, then on to George Deaderick in 1803, and later to Jacob McGavock. This old townhouse let's us see some real old history of Nashville.

There have been many other wonderful mansions in Nashville that have been torn down. There were some beautiful homes in the Edgefield section of East Nashville. Some homes there have been renovated. Back in its time, Edgefield was quite an elite area.

During the 19th century, one of the largest and most impressive mansions in Nashville was **Oak Hill**, the home of Van Leer Kirkman. Today, the First Presbyterian Church occupies that site at the corner of Franklin Pike and Tyne Boulevard.

There were wonderful homes on old Rutledge Hill south of downtown Nashville. There is one old home still standing there.

Sometime you might want to do a little tour hopping of these and other old Nashville mansions.

Good to the Last Drop

In the 1800s, John Overton, owner of Traveller's Rest, purchased the land at the corner of Church Street and Fourth Avenue, North (then called Cherry Street) and started construction on his vision of a grand hotel, the Maxwell House Hotel. Overton named the hotel in honor of his wife, whose name was Mary Maxwell Overton.

Only a portion of the hotel was finished before the interruption of the Civil War. The portion that had been completed served as Confederate barracks and a storehouse prior to Nashville's capture. Following capture, the partially built Maxwell House Hotel was used by the Union forces as a hospital and prison.

After the war, John Overton's son, John Overton, Jr. (The Colonel) took over his father's financial empire and completed the building of the hotel at a cost of $250,000, which was a tremendous sum of money for that time. The grand hotel was opened on September 22, 1869.

I have glorious memories of that grand, historic hotel standing on the corner where the Sun Trust Bank Building stands today.

Before the hotel burned in 1961, the grand hotel served many famous people. One such guest was the renowned writer, William Sydney Porter, who went by the name O. Henry. He enjoyed his stay at the hotel so much that he began to write a short story about the hotel and Nashville while crossing the Cumberland River railroad bridge as he departed the city. He titled his short story *A Municipal Report*.

Eight presidents of the United States were guests at the old Maxwell House.

The Cheek-Neal Company named their coffee after the name of the hotel. While on a visit to Nashville, President Theodore Roosevelt was served Maxwell House coffee at a breakfast at The Hermitage. President Roosevelt referred to the cup of coffee as "good to the last drop." This slogan started an advertising campaign for the coffee which still exists today.

Over the years, just a few of the other prominent guests registering at the Maxwell House were Otis Skinner, Sarah Bernhardt, Enrico Caruso when he came to sing in Nashville, Henry Ford, Thomas Edison, William Jennings Bryan, and John Phillip Sousa.

As a professional musician from the 1940s on, I have wonderful memories of the hotel's grandeur. Dressed in my tuxedo, I felt such dignity as I walked from the ornate lobby up the plush, grand staircase with its carved railings. The open, stately staircase led to the lavish mezzanine just outside the ballroom where generals and presidents had strolled overlooking the lobby.

I remember seeing the elegant mass of Nashville ladies fashioned in their gorgeous dresses, and the men well-groomed in their tuxedos or white ties and tails.

Walking into the ballroom held us in awe as we gazed upon its spaciousness, the high ceiling, its eloquent columns, and its tasteful decorativeness.

Thousands of dinners and dances were held in the elegant ballroom by sororities, fraternities, Cotillion Clubs, Bachelors Clubs, conventions, business meetings, and many other organizations from the city.

Some of the local dance orchestras that played those dinner-dances may have been orchestras of leaders Horace Holley, Adrian McDowell, Owen Bradley, Tommy Knowles, Bill Yandle, Red McEwen, Tom Hewgley, Neill Owen, Bob "Hamp" Young, Fred Shoemake, Papa John Gordy, David Sunstead, or Charles Nagy, to mention a few.

Prior to this period in Nashville, the orchestras might have been Francis Craig, Beasley Smith, Jimmy Gallagher, Vito Pellettiere, or Tony Rose. Incidentally, Phil Harris played drums in Tony Rose's orchestra during the 1920s, and Charlie Barnet played saxophone in Beasley Smith's orchestra prior to forming his own band. During my time, Vito Pellettiere became the WSM radio's music librarian and eventually stage manager for the *Grand Ole Opry*.

These are my memories of the Maxwell House Hotel during that Golden Age of the Big Bands. Most musicians still carry a youthful spirit into old age. We lived through too much greatness to be otherwise.

Each day, many political, professional, and business leaders could be seen eating at the Maxwell House Coffee Shop.

I remember seeing an advertisement in an old Nashville newspaper where the old Maxwell House at Fourth and Church in its earlier days was "serving their regular Sunday style dinners every Thursday night from 5 until 9 for $1.00." The ad stated that the dinners were especially priced for "family and party groups."

At Christmas time of 1961, the Maxwell House Hotel caught on fire and burned out of control. From that time on, all we have are our memories.

Maxwell House Hotel after fire, 1961

Songs of Faith Ring Again from Tulip Street

Among many historic structures which are prevalent in our historic Athens of the South, one of the sights all Nashvillians should see is Tulip Street United Methodist Church located in East Nashville.

Before the beginning of the Civil War, the congregation of Tulip Street was organized in 1859. The original church building was located on Tulip Street (which today we call Fifth Street) in Edgefield, then an affluent suburban satellite city near Nashville.

Thirty years later, to accommodate the continuing growth of the church, plans were made to relocate and build at the corner of Sixth and Russell Streets. That church still stands on that corner today. The cornerstone of the building was laid in 1891, with completion and dedication in 1892.

Tulip Street has seen the Civil War, two cholera epidemics, the East Nashville fire of 1916, and three tornadoes. The most recent disaster to strike this historic congregation was the April 1998 tornado. That recent storm demolished the entire east wall of the sanctuary, but left the rest of the sanctuary's interior unscathed.

Donations began to pour in to rebuild the sanctuary wall which included many beautiful stained-glass windows. While rebuilding, the congregation continued to worship in the sanctuary. Stained-glass pieces recovered from the original windows were used in the newly constructed windows.

My family and I attended the Sunday worship service when the new stained-glass windows were dedicated. They are beautiful and spiritually uplifting. Also, decorative terra-cotta moldings were crafted to return the building's exterior to its original character.

An historical brochure published by the Tulip Street congregation proudly states: "Many architectural experts regard Tulip Street's sanctuary as the finest example of Neo-Romanesque architecture in the Nashville area, characterized by rounded arches, vaulted ceilings, and the extensive use of terra-cotta, hard-baked pottery moldings that are well illustrated on the building's exterior."

The church's pipe organ is one of the few tracker pipe organs in existence. The organ which stands in the sanctuary today was built by Jardine and Sons of New York, and installed in 1892. In a tracker organ, air is released from the air chambers into the pipes manually each time a key is depressed.

My family and I were able to enjoy this wonderful organ for more than four years when I served the church as its choir director back during the 1960s. Long-time church member Frances Southerland was the fine organist.

The bell tower atop the building suspends the Tennessee Centennial Bells. This collection of ten bells were first used in 1897 during the Tennessee Centennial Exposition in Nashville's West Side Park which now we call Centennial Park. The bells were purchased and relocated to Tulip Street's Church tower after the Centennial Exposition celebration.

Although the church's bell tower sustained the high winds of the April, 1998 tornado, there resulted some serious structural damage. The church made plans to dismantle and reconstruct the bell tower brick by brick so that these historic bells could once again ring out songs of faith over the entire Edgefield community of East Nashville.

Tulip Street's cultural history and enrichment is another significant piece of our Athens of the South.

Tulip Street Methodist Church

Old Nashville Family Names

It is interesting to note how many old family names identifying many descendants from the Old Nashville are still living in the Nashville area.

I met at least two of these descendants of Nashville's historic figures when I taught the six-weeks class on "Nashville Nostalgia" at Vanderbilt in their "Retirement Learning at Vanderbilt" series.

Mr. Walter Hardcastle, a participant in the class sessions, revealed to us that he was a distant relative of Lucinda "Granny" White. Another participant in the classes was Mrs. Harriet Jones Doermann who is a great-great-granddaughter of Reverend William Hume who was a religious and educational leader in Nashville, and the father of Alfred Hume who was the first superintendent of Nashville public schools.

Soon after that class session when we met Harriet Jones Doermann, I walked into my church and saw my friend, Edgar Jones. Edgar said, "My aunt was telling me a lot about your classes at Vanderbilt." Then, he said, "Harriet is my aunt. She and my father are brother and sister."

Well, that means that Edgar is a descendant of the Hume family, too. You can imagine how many descendants of Old Nashville families are still living in our midst.

Tennessee was first a portion of North Carolina. In 1778, James Robertson scouted our Nashville area with eight other men. The next year, Robertson returned with approximately 250 people to build a permanent settlement here.

We still honor his family by naming the James Robertson Parkway for his name. Our Charlotte Avenue is named for Charlotte Robertson, the wife of James. Many Robertsons today bear their relationship. The descendants of General James Robertson had a family reunion in Nashville in 2001. It was reported that a large number of descendants attended the reunion.

A partner of James Robertson named Colonel John Donelson brought some families over 1,000 miles by river boats down the Holston, Tennessee, Ohio, and Cumberland rivers arriving in April of 1780 to these Cumberland Bluffs. I would have to imagine that descendents of Donelson still live in our midst.

McGavock has been a name of distinction in Nashville almost since the beginning. The earliest map of Nashville was drawn by a surveyor, David McGavock, when Nashville was only six years old. The McGavocks were noted for building some very nice homes in the area.

Just before the Civil War, David H. McGavock built the **Two Rivers Mansion** which stands out in Donelson on McGavock Pike. David's wife was Willie Harding, a daughter of Belle Meade's plantation owner, William Harding. He gave Willie a track of land on which she and her husband, David, built Two Rivers mansion.

Randall McGavock built his home in Franklin, Tennessee and named it **Carnton** after their old family home in Ireland. A good part of the Civil War in this area highlights Carnton's history.

Lysander McGavock built his home called **Midway**. This fine home was halfway between Nashville and Franklin. Now, this gracious old home is the Brentwood Country Club on Franklin Pike.

Jacob McGavock built his home on Cherry Street (Fourth Avenue, North) in Nashville located about 200 feet from where the old Maxwell House Hotel later would stand. Jacob McGavock had joined two great Nashville names by marrying the daughter of Felix Grundy.

Philip Lindsley served as the president of the old University of Nashville. He married Sarah McGavock, the daughter of Jacob.

Just think of how many local descendants of the old Bellevue families probably still live in the Nashville area. There would be descendants of DeMoss, Carter, Davis, Newsom, Howe, Hooten, and Hicks, among others.

I like to think that my ancestors go back quite a way in the development of this area.

My great-great-grandfather on my father's side was Reverend Miles Eddings Johnston. He was a devoted family man and a Methodist preacher.

My father's grandparents were James Thomas Ellis and Louisia Parlee Johnston Ellis. They lived in a small town called Shop Springs, Tennessee, not far from Watertown, Tennessee. My first name is Ellis which is my grandmother's maiden name. The following story was passed down to us by our relatives from the Ellis side of the family, George Horne and Effie Lovett, now living in Columbia, TN.

Back in the old days, a farmer would load up a wagon with fruit, vegetables, shoes, lamps, oil, household items, and other materials. He would hook his horse to the wagon, and slowly move through the area selling his wares.

Lamps were the only source of light people had in those days. Everyone needed oil to keep their lamps burning.

In the vicinity of Shop Springs, there were several small churches nestled among the rolling hills of our beautiful Tennessee. All of the churches, just like the homes in Shop Springs, depended on oil lamps.

Every Sunday morning when people arrived at their various churches, they were amazed to find that all of their lamps were full of oil and had been turned on. No one could find out who was filling all of those lamps with oil.

Finally, one day the mystery was solved. When my great-grandfather, James Ellis, died of a heart attack at age sixty-five, all of the church people realized that the lamps were left empty. James Ellis never revealed his good deeds to these church members, but he was no longer able to keep the lamps full of oil.

In later years, many of my father's family moved to West Nashville. This included my grandmother, Callie Ellis Thompson, and my grandfather, William Nathaniel Thompson. The family, of course, included my father, his brother and sister.

My mother's family was the Dillinghams. We own a genealogy of the Dillinghams, and they are traced all the way back from England, to America, and into Tennessee.

Back in the old days in the hills west of Nashville, a number of communities developed over the years known as Harpeth Ridge. Some settled communities were Watkins Grove, Ezell Hollow, Dozier, Overall Creek, Pegram, Newsom Station, Kingston Springs, Shacklett, Linton, Pasquo, and Bellevue.

The Dillingham family had long been residents of the Dog Creek Narrows of Harpeth community. William Winn Dillingham was my great-grandfather on my mother's side.

His children began moving into the West Nashville area. One of his children was George Joshua Dillingham. He was my grandfather. He married Susie Amanda Whitfield who was my grandmother.

My grandparents on my mother's side of the family had six children, 5 girls and 1 boy. One of their daughters was Blanche Hutton Dillingham. She married Ellis Dillard Thompson Senior. They were my mother and father.

And, my wife has this interesting story of her relatives in Nashville. My wife's grandfather was Timothy Hampton Moore. Back in the old days, he was part owner of Moore and Hadley Buggy and Harness Company in Nashville.

He had a fine business and was very successful as his products and services were needed by many. However, when the automobile was invented and came on the scene, people told Tim, "You had better include autos and auto parts in your business."

Tim said, "Oh, that fad will never catch on. Automobiles won't last."

Famous last words! Autos not only became popular, but grandfather Tim Moore lost his buggy and harness business, and lost all of his money.

Tim Moore was the father of my wife's mother, Frances Adaline Moore Young.

My wife thinks that in the old days, her grandparents, the Tim Moores, had their home out on that old road which today runs beside the Cool Springs area, and that is why it is named Moores Lane.

Old Nashville
Through the Eyes of a Boy

Still a boy's spirit caught in the present,
but pulled relentlessly back toward the past.

Clemons School

Remembering the Steps I Took to School

From my first year of school through the sixth grade, I attended Clemons School on Twelfth Avenue, South. The school is no longer there.

As children, we often walked to and from school from our homes on Paris Avenue. This was in the early 1930s. I would not recommend that children walk the streets anywhere today without protection.

The other day, I slowly drove my car from Paris Avenue up Twelfth Avenue to Ashwood Avenue. This was the trip we took when walking to and from school.

The old neighborhood has changed. Recently, Metro has put in new sidewalks on Twelfth Avenue, South, and new attractive street lamp posts have been installed which help the appearance of the area.

Thinking back, I remember the four corners at Twelfth and Paris. One corner was a vacant lot. On another corner was an H. G. Hill Store. I was told that Stephens & Jordan Grocery was on another corner which today is the site of the 21st Century Christian Bookstore. I always called it the Harris Grocery store. As a small child, I guess a Mr. Harris must have worked there who always helped me. On the fourth corner was a filling station. The filling station sold gas for 19 cents a gallon. People pumped their own gas while watching the gas slowly go down in the large container at the top of the pump.

Next to Harris or Stephens Grocery on Twelfth Avenue was the home of the Sears family. They had a blacksmith shop out back, and a livery stable.

Moving on up to the corner of Twelfth and Dallas Avenues, there was the greatest drugstore in the world for a kid walking home from school.

I remember Manning's Drugstore for its marble soda fountain, the ceiling fans, and the prescription counter where we would see bottles of Lydia E. Pinkham Compound, Carter's Little Liver Pills, and the dreaded Dr. Caldwell's Syrup of Pepsin.

I remember the glassed-in candy case. For just a few pennies, we could buy a jaw breaker, some jelly beans, some Necco candy wafers, and a stick of licorice. Much too expensive for us were those attractive boxes of Belle Camp chocolates on display.

The drugstore sold our school supplies such as pencils, erasers, and our Blue Horse notebooks. The old Manning's Drugstore is today the site of the Corner Music Store.

Across the street from Manning's, at the corner of Twelfth and Halcyon Avenues, was Lester's Grocery. We went to school with Harry Lester who later served as one of our noted judges for many years.

On that same side of Twelfth Avenue was a pie wagon, and the old Tidwell's Grocery Store. I have distinct memories of that store. During The Great Depression of the early 1930s, my father was laid off from his job at the railroad. Once in a while, his name would come up on the "extra board" which gave him a day or night to work here and there. But, during that period of time, my father worked as the butcher at Tidwell's Grocery.

I remember the old butcher shop area of the store had sawdust on the floor, a large meat cutting block, and a scary assortment of cleavers and knives.

Back in those hard-time days, many grocery customers would say, "I'll have to let my bill run."

The grocer would say, "O. K., I'll carry you."

The customer would say, "On pay day, I'll catch it up."

That was the familiar dialogue of the day.

On that same side of the street at the corner of Twelfth and Montrose Avenues, was Becker's Bakery. Would you believe, the exact store is still there.

The bakery was founded in 1925. To my great amazement and joy, they still make the same sweet rolls with raisins that our daddy often brought home for us to eat. I have eaten some recently, and those sweet rolls are made by the same exact recipe of more than seventy years ago at Becker's Bakery.

As I slowly drove the car on toward Clemons School, we came to the corner of Twelfth and Sweetbriar. I remember a gas station being there. That corner still has a transmission repair shop on it.

Then, we came to Twelfth and Beechwood Avenues. On the corner, there used to be the Waverly-Belmont Church of Christ. A church is still there. Now, it is the Zion Hill First African Baptist Church. I am glad the building still stands.

The next corner we came to was Twelfth and Elmwood Avenues. There was an H. G. Hill Store there. Next to the store was a small barbershop. I used to get my haircuts there sometimes. The barber was Mr. Talley who went to our church. Across the street was an ice house.

At Twelfth and Linden Avenues was where we stopped when we got out of school. Sewell's Drugstore on the corner was a good place to get bubble gum and our baseball trading cards. That corner is now occupied by a floral shop.

Clemons School sat between Linden and Ashwood Avenues. The school is gone. There are a few houses built in that area now. But, remnants of the old concrete steps from the sidewalk which led up to the doors of the school are still there.

The old school steps, and my many steps to and from school will be lasting memories.

Becker's Bakery

There Used to Be a Train Depot Right Here

Frank Sinatra sang a song, "There Used to Be a Ball Park Right Here." I could sing, "There Used to Be a Train Depot Right Here."

My life and trains go back many years. The Union Station Hotel in Nashville is bulging with memories of when it was a train depot. My father worked for the railroad for many years. My uncle used to be the barber in the Union Station barbershop.

The old Nashville Union Station was built in 1900, and served as the city's train station until the 1970s. It was unused until it reopened as a grand hotel in 1986.

Soon after the old depot had been shaped into a hotel, I stepped in off of Broad Street one day and enjoyed seeing the Grand Hotel with its attractive grill work around the many staircases that carved their way up and around the five floors which were visible from the lobby. The lobby reaches 63 feet from the floor to the stained-glass panes in the ceiling.

I saw the ornate sky light glowing with its sunny brilliance over the entire lobby. One could be awe struck by the beauty of the enormous amount of gold leaf, the ancient style columns, and the decorative workmanship from the floor to the ceiling.

The gracious old limestone fireplace was still there. One of the old train station entrances had been converted into a glassed-in restaurant. One of the old depot waiting rooms had become part of the ballroom. The carpeting in the lobby was adorned with shades of color which complimented the walls.

There was beautiful furniture where the old ticket windows used to be. And, my heart almost stopped beating when I came to the alcove that used to be the barbershop. I had to sit down in one of the soft, cushioned chairs where the old barbershop waiting chairs used to sit. For a few moments, I just sat and reflected on years gone by.

My uncle, Mr. Lawrence Owens, who was affectionately known as Tony, used to cut hair in a chair about ten feet from where I was sitting. In fact, I sat in that chair when he gave me my first shave back when I was fifteen years old. My uncle must have seen a little peach fuzz growing on my face.

That quaint, old barbershop alcove had been transformed into a luxurious room covered with a rug running to the outside edge of the marble tile floor. Green plants in beautiful holders were situated where the old barber chair used to be. There was a large, oil painting on the back wall enhanced by indirect lighting. Uncle Lawrence wouldn't believe how the old barbershop had changed.

My family rode trains all during my childhood. My father, who went by Ed Thompson, worked as a foreman in the yards for the L & N (Louisville and Nashville) railroad, and the N C & St L (Nashville, Chattanooga, and St. Louis) railroad.

Back in 1930, when our nation was suffering from The Great Depression, I was six years old. Since my father worked for the railroad, he was able to get free passes for his whole family to ride the passenger trains when we wanted to take a trip. We traveled to Louisville, Cincinnati, Miami, to the Chicago World's Fair, to Dallas, Texas for the Pan American Exposition, and all points between.

I always enjoyed riding the trains and reading the time tables. I knew where all of the towns and stops were located. No wonder I was so good in geography class over in Clemons School on Twelfth Avenue in South Nashville.

My family especially enjoyed taking the train up to Louisville, Kentucky. Back during the 1930s, my mother, father, sister, and I could spend an all-day trip to Louisville for about two dollars.

On a Saturday morning, we could get up very early, dress, and walk to the depot in downtown Nashville. My mother would pack a lunch basket with a lot of good sandwiches, deviled eggs, pickles, and fruit. We could buy cold drinks for a nickel, or we could just drink water.

I knew every train station between Nashville and Louisville. Some we stopped at, some we didn't.

When we arrived in Louisville, we would take a streetcar to Fountain Ferry Park. What a thrill. My sister and I would ride the merry-go-round and play on the swings. We would walk around and look at people and interesting sights. Then, when we got hungry, we would eat our sandwiches.

When it started getting late, we would get on back to the Louisville depot and wait for the train to head back to Nashville.

Getting on the train feeling happy but tired, we would get four seats together on the coach, and turn two of the seats facing the other two. For a few minutes, we would sit and reflect on what a great time we had in Louisville. Then, because we were so terribly tired, we would shut our eyes and doze off, or sleep, or just think.

One of the most enjoyable and peaceful feelings in the world was to doze off to the rhythmic sound of the "clickity-clack" of the wheels going over the rails. The lights would be dim. Only the sound of the conductor coming through the coach to check the tickets, or to call out a station, would interrupt the hypnotic, rhythmic power of the wheels below moving through the countryside.

When we arrived at our Union Station, we were tired and sleepy, but filled with the memories of a wonderful day. That day would always be remembered as a family day of happiness.

———◦———

It seems like the only thing which remains the same is change!

In October of 2000, I went back to the old Union Station for a tour and the celebration of the 100th anniversary of the old building sponsored by Historic Nashville, Inc. I was shocked to see that even more changes had been made to the present grand hotel.

And, since that time, we have seen the old, historic train shed torn down, and the side carriage entrance has been altered.

Today, all of us can enjoy the magnificence of the Union Station Hotel in Nashville, but my mind also remembers and hears the shout, "All aboard!" Because, there used to be a train depot right here.

Union Station

Are You Going to the Car Barn?

Nashville's old streetcar barn, sometimes called the shed, was downtown along with the Transfer Station. This great old meeting place was in the block bounded by Deaderick Street, Third Avenue, Fourth Avenue, and Cedar Street (which we now call Charlotte Avenue.)

The streetcars were operated by the Nashville Railway and Light Company. You could ride any car on any line, go to the Transfer Station, get a transfer, and get on any other car headed to any other destination for no extra charge.

Maybe you remember some of the car lines we could take. There were streetcars named Hillsboro, West End, Kane Avenue, Glendale, Porter Road, Jefferson Street, Waverly, Nolensville Road, Fatherland Street, Belmont Heights, and many more.

If you ever caught a car in the Transfer Station, I am sure you remember going through the turnstiles. I remember the long, hard benches for waiting passengers which were near the food and drink concessions.

When our desired streetcar showed up, we would rush to get on the car to get a seat by the window. However, I stood while riding many times. My mother taught me that if the car was crowded and a lady got on, I was to tip my hat and give her my seat.

When I was small, I had to hold on to the brass handle on the back of the seats when I had to stand in the aisle. But, adults could reach the leather straps hanging down from the ceiling of the car.

I always liked to hear the motorman stomp on a metal plate on the floor to ring the bell. It served as a horn for pedestrians or autos that got in the way of the streetcar.

Most of my experience was on the old Belmont Heights streetcars. When we would go to a movie downtown at night, we would rush out from the theatre to catch the first Belmont car to take us home. With one foot on the step of the car entrance, we would ask the motorman, "Are you going to the car barn?"

If so, then that was his last run for the night. He would take the car to the barn and leave it. If he said that he was not going to the car barn, then we would pile on. The car would go west on Church Street, turn left on to Eighth Avenue, and then right on Broadway. The car would go down to Twelfth Avenue and turn left. We would be heading out to Belmont Heights and home.

The old Belmont line ended at Cedar Lane. Sometimes I would walk up to Cedar Lane to get on the streetcar to go to town. For the car to head in the opposite direction on the tracks, the motorman would have to switch the trolley to the other end of the car, and connect it to the electric cable above. Also, he would walk down the aisle and turn all of the seats the opposite direction so people would be riding looking toward the front of the car.

Another association I had with streetcars was when a bunch of us in the neighborhood would walk the streetcar tracks out to the old area of Glendale Park and the Glendale Zoo in South Nashville.

Historical Marker at Glendale & Lealand Lanes

The End of the Line Was Glendale Park

At the end of the line in this part of South Nashville, the Nashville Railway and Light Company, who were the owners and operators of the city's streetcars, built a sixty-four acre amusement park and zoo.

For a little history, the park opened in 1888 to attract passengers for the railway. Railway was the correct term, because originally, the streetcars were run by steam. They became electric streetcars in 1893. The Glendale Zoo was added to the park in 1912.

Glendale Park was located roughly around our present Glendale Lane and Lealand Lane area. The prese Lealand Lane heading out from town is where the streetc tracks were.

As kids, we used to enjoy starting around Kirkwo Lane and walking the streetcar tracks out to the old p area. In those days, there was nothing on each side of t tracks but Brown's Creek and the woods.

The old Glendale streetcar would go out to the pa make a big rounding turn on the tracks, and then head back to town. Close to our present Glendale Lane off of Lealand Lane is where the streetcar made its big turn.

We went to the Agriculture Building, and spent a large amount of time in the Woman's Building. There we saw blue ribbons for everything from flowers to preserves to quilts.

I still wanted to go on over to the Midway and go on some of the rides, but actually I had some fun collecting various give-away items. We always left with a free yard stick, ruler, paint stirrer, a card of sewing needles, some pencils, and many more things which we didn't need!

The one mile oval, dirt race track within the fairgrounds had harness racing every day. When we finally got to go to the Midway, we either crossed the race track when it was clear, or walked through the tunnel which was built under the track.

When we finally arrived at the Midway, we rode the whip, the Ferris wheel, the merry-go-round, and other rides. I had no desire to get on the Big Dipper which was a wooden roller coaster. That was a permanent ride at Cumberland Park. It was torn down some time ago.

In the Midway we heard all of the sideshow barkers telling us what strange and magnificent things we would see if we bought a ticket and came inside the tent.

There were games where you would try to win a kewpie doll. Your money could disappear fast when you couldn't throw something, hit something, hook something, ring some dishes, or execute some other feat of skill.

Of course, adults could also lose money trying to see if the carnival man could guess their age or weight. Today, that would not be politically correct to have a man tell a lady that she weighed 185 pounds!

The smell of the hamburgers and onions cooking could get to you, too. Various civic and church organizations had tents where they served food to make money for their organizations. We always ate at one of the Methodist Church tents.

Then, it was time to get some seats in the grandstand to watch the free acts. The fair presented great circus acts, clowns, animals, and other professional acts. Following the free acts, there was a loud explosion, and the fireworks display had begun.

Every night we could hear the fireworks even if we were at home. Sometimes a neighbor would take a bunch of us kids and drive over to a hill in the fairgrounds area where we could see the fireworks.

In 1965, the stately old grandstand as well as the administration building and some of the exhibition buildings burned. The buildings were replaced, but with structures which didn't have that same old character and charm as the originals.

In later years, as a musician, I had the opportunity to play some of the grandstand acts. Over in what we called the Fairgrounds Coliseum, I had the opportunity to play the horse show which was presented each night of the fair. Also, the Shrine Circus used to play in that building. In 1970, the Fairgrounds Coliseum burned, and it was never rebuilt.

The fair was truly a state fair. It was a good place for the FHA, FFA, 4-H Clubs, and other student organizations to show off their year long work. We need a lot more healthy organizations and events like those today to occupy the minds and bodies of our youth.

The Old Knot Hole Gang

As the baseball games appear on television, and the World Series draws near, every Knot Hole Kid in Nashville is swept back to the baseball memories of his or her youth.

I know that my memories will take me back to old Sulphur Dell ballpark which used to stand at Fifth Avenue, North. Our new Bi-Centennial Mall has now taken over that general area north of the state capitol building.

Why the name Sulphur Dell? That is the location where James Robertson and the first settlers arrived in Nashville. It was the Sulphur Springs Bottom. Sulphur water was abundant. I remember my family often going to Morgan Park near the Dell carrying two or three jugs to take some good sulphur water back home.

The first person to call the Sulphur Springs Bottom ballpark by the sporty name of Sulphur Dell was a legendary, local sports writer for *The Tennessean* by the name of Grantland Rice.

The Nashville Vols baseball team during my young years was managed by Larry Gilbert. More than a half century later, I can still tell you some of the players on the team when I watched the games. Mickey Rocco played first base, Johnny Mahalic was the second baseman. After playing ball, Johnny went on to be a big executive at Vultee Aircraft, later to be called Avco.

Buster Boguskie was the well-liked shortstop. Buster, an East Nashville boy, served many years on the Metro Council after his baseball years.

Of course, there was the great ball player, Charlie Gilbert, son of manager Larry Gilbert. Charlie went on to play in the major leagues. I remember the catcher, Smokey Burgess. There was a pitcher by the name of Boots Poffenberger whom I enjoyed watching, and another fine pitcher was George Jeffcoat. And, who could ever forget the umpire behind the plate? Everybody liked Steamboat Johnson.

I remember that after the seventh inning at many games, the owners would open a big gate on the wall out near right field. All of the kids were allowed to go in free and stand to watch the last couple of innings. They called the group the Knot Hole Gang. How great it was when the game went into extra innings.

The old double-A Southern Association back then had eight teams. In addition to the Nashville Vols, we had the Memphis Chicks, the Chattanooga Lookouts, the Birmingham Barons, the New Orleans Pelicans, and Atlanta back then was a minor league team. They were called the Atlanta Crackers. The Little Rock Travelers and Mobile Bears were the other two teams.

I have additional memories about Sulphur Dell. Being a musician, I got to play the Tom Pack Circus in the Dell which was the Shrine Circus at the time. Also, once a water show came into the Dell which hired a local band. At that time, I was playing with the Red McEwen Orchestra which played many of the shows which came to town.

Also, on some of the opening days at the ball park in April, a live band was hired to play during the game.

So much for memories.

Nashville's historic baseball park was the oldest stadium in the United States when the last ballgame was played there in 1963.

There is one great thing about growing old. We may not get to see and do the same things we used to, but for sure, we can always keep the memories. Play ball!

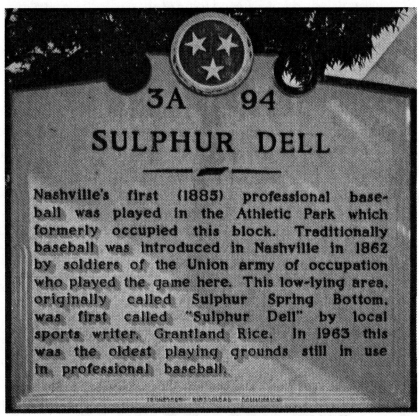

Historical Marker near Bi-Centennial Mall

"I'll Meet You on Fifth Avenue"

Back in the late 1930s and early 1940s when I grew up in Nashville, our favorite past-time was to take a streetcar to the downtown shopping and theatre district which was mainly Church Street and Fifth Avenue plus the surrounding area.

Downtown was the center of all the activity and excitement. There were no shopping malls, so all of the shopping took place downtown. The Five & Ten Cent stores were there. The soda shops and drugstores were abundant. There were six movie theatres downtown around Church Street plus a stage show always at one of them. And, Fifth Avenue was where we could run into just about everybody we knew.

Let me take you on a trip back to the old Fifth Avenue between Church Street and Union Street of my growing years, and see how Fifth Avenue has changed today.

Back in the old days, on the west side of Fifth Avenue starting at Church Street we had the Cain-Sloan Company. This was where it was before Harvey's took in the whole block of Church Street, and also before Cain-Sloan moved across Church Street re-locating from the corner of Fifth Avenue down to the McKendree Methodist Church.

Of course, Cain-Sloan is now gone completely. However, the old Cain-Sloan corner at Fifth and Church is still called St. Cloud's Corner. During the Civil War, this corner was the location of a hotel called the St. Cloud House.

Also, on the west side of Fifth Avenue, we had four Five & Ten Cent stores. We had Grant's, Woolworth, McLellan's, and Kress.

If we walk or drive down Fifth Avenue today, we will see that the old W. T. Grant Company location is now The Arts Company. The F. W. Woolworth building is now the Dollar General Store. Our old McLellan's building is now the Family Dollar store.

The last time I walked down Fifth Avenue, the old S. H. Kress & Company's five-story building was vacant. But, on the top floor of the old building, we can still see the gold letters spelling the word KRESS.

On that block of Fifth Avenue between Church and Union there were other small shops, too. I remember a hat shop, the Fox dress shop, and Baker's shoe store.

At the corner of Fifth Avenue and Union Street was the lovely Loveman, Berger & Teitlebaum department store. We just called it Loveman's. Today at that corner is Franklin's Printing and Office Supply Company which stands within the larger structure called The Five Hundred and One Union Building.

Over on the east side of Fifth Avenue in this block between Church Street and Union Street, starting up at the Church Street corner, I can remember a tobacco shop, an Orange Juice Bar, a Krystal at some time, and E. Lee Bennett's optometrist office.

There were two movie theatres on that side of the street. We had the Rex Theatre and the Fifth Avenue

Theatre. Most of that area today is taken up by the Sun Trust Bank Building.

Next to the Arcade, there was always a drugstore. Even today, there is a Walgreens Drugstore next to the Arcade.

There were some other shops on that same side of Fifth Avenue between the Arcade and Union Street. It seems like I remember a dress shop, a linen shop, a hat shop, and a Family Booterie.

Old Fifth Avenue of today doesn't look the same. Today, the main things we would miss, in addition to the stores and theatres mentioned, would be the happy clamor of the crowds of Nashvillians busily shopping, waving at friends, and eating popcorn from one of the Five & Ten Cent stores or hot cashew nuts from The Peanut Shop in the Arcade. There was the opportunity of placing some change in the hat of a couple of singers and guitar players sitting on the sidewalk who were less fortunate than we.

Today, we would miss all of that plus the screaming when we saw someone we knew, pulling a new item out of the sack to show our friend what we had just bought, and deciding where we would go for a refreshing cold drink, ice cream soda, or maybe buy tickets to a movie.

Those old streetcars took us to an exciting world which we called downtown. It was the world of department stores, Five & Ten Cent stores, lunch places, theatres, and people. A Saturday journey into this old world meant greeting and meeting, shopping and eating.

Boys made sure that their hair was combed. Girls were so neat in their nice dresses, dainty little hats, and wrist-length white gloves.

I can remember old Fifth Avenue and smile. In thinking back to those old days, I miss my friends calling me and saying, "I'll meet you on Fifth Avenue."

*Downtown shoppers caught by candid camerman,
EDT and mother, c. 1940*

In the Good Old Summertime

When I was growing up, the good old summertime always meant heading to the swimming pool.

It may mean the same to people today. However, because the culture of society has changed so much, "off to the swimming pool" today may mean to go over to the club house and pool built within our own development area.

It may mean going in the pool at the hotel or motel on our next out-of-town trip.

It may mean going to the pool at the country club.

If you are so fortunate, it may mean going in your pool in the back yard.

Today, to my family sometimes, it means going to one of the Family YMCA pools which are very nice and have well-trained lifeguards.

Back when I was growing up in Nashville, there were many swimming pools scattered about the city. The city government built and maintained many pools for its citizens.

The kids in my neighborhood traveled mainly to four outstanding swimming pools. As my mind begins to swim with memories, let me tell you about them.

Before my father got sick and bedridden, he used to take us out to the Centennial Park pool. I practiced the swimming requirements for my Eagle Scout merit badge there. My dad stayed outside of the fence, pulled his old railroad pocket watch from his vest, and timed me as I swam back and forth across the pool.

A number of years ago, the city filled in the pool in Centennial Park and converted it to a very attractive Art Center which stands at that site today.

The Centennial Art Center displays nice plants, greenery, flowers, outside tables for meetings, and an air-conditioned art gallery.

You can still stand on the concrete edge where the pool used to be and visualize the cool blue water, the crowd of joyous bathers, the screaming of the children, and the happy music coming out of the loud speakers. Of course, we are proud of the Art Center which is there today.

Also, back in those days, we kids enjoyed going to the great pool in Shelby Park (whenever we could get somebody to drive us across town.) At night the Shelby Park pool had beautiful lights under the water which made for a nice appearance. Also, the pool was heated for us to enjoy at night.

After World War II, many of us often traveled down to Franklin to go swimming at Willow Plunge. What a delightful pool that was with the green grass slopping down to the water, and a popular song of the day played by a big, name band coming out of the loud speakers. Today, old Willow Plunge has been covered over, and new homes are built on top of that area.

And then, there was Cascade Plunge. It was located within the area of the state fairgrounds not far from Nolensville Road. Cascade Plunge derived its name from the waterfalls and cascades spilling out into the giant pool. There was an area for children, a middle size area, and the large, deep area where the diving boards and even a high tower were located.

Les Jameson, who used to be a radio talk show host at WLAC before his death, was a lifeguard at Cascade Plunge back in the old days.

I remember that the first frozen candy bar I experienced was from the concession stand at Cascade Plunge. I always got a frozen Powerhouse candy bar. It was like a chocolate jaw breaker. It is a wonder that any of us ever had teeth.

We don't have those same pools today. However, our Metropolitan government still has and maintains about 14 pools which are free or low-cost for today's citizens.

Or, one can take advantage of the very nice Wave Pool in Donelson, Pleasant Green out Gallatin Road, Nashville Shores on Bell Road, and others.

Today, all of the park pools are open to anyone with swimming lessons provided free of charge. The Family YMCA pools and the pool at the Jewish Community Center are open to all family members regardless of race, creed or national origin.

"Did Anyone Empty the Pan?"

Some young people might say, "Wow, you really had it rough back in those old days!"

When I came up as a boy, more than three-quarters of a century ago, we didn't have a lot of the machines, devices, or certainly the high-tech that we enjoy today.

We didn't have a dish washer. My mother hand washed every dish and every kitchen utensil in a dish pan with soap and hot water. Often, I was the one to take a dish towel and dry each piece.

We didn't have a washing machine. Clothes were washed in a large wash tub by scrubbing each piece on a wash board with soap and hot water which had been heated on the stove.

We had no electric dryer. All clothes and bedding were stretched out on a clothes line to dry in the purity of the hot and natural sunshine. The clean and fragrant smell was a delight to our nostrils.

We had no electric refrigerator to store food. We had an icebox. The ice man came through the neighborhood often in his horse-drawn wagon to sell us ice. We could get a 25 pound block of ice for a dime.

One side of the icebox was used to store the food and keep it cold. The other side of the box contained the block of ice.

The icebox did create one problem. When the ice melted, the water dripped down into a pan at the bottom of the icebox near the floor. Many times when my family would be away from the house, someone would remember and yell, "Did anyone remember to empty the pan?"

We had a telephone. To make a call, we had to talk to the operator and give her the number we wished to call. The phone bill was far cheaper if one had a 2, 3, or 4-party line. We had to listen for our particular ring before answering the phone. And, it was very unethical to listen in on another party's phone conversation.

Television had hardly been thought of back then. But, radios were important. I remember when my daddy and I built a crystal set, and we could pick up WSM over the ear phones. We later got a Majestic radio for the living room on which all of us could hear a favorite program as we sat together and stared at the radio during the program.

Automobiles were important, too. Of course, autos came without starters. We had to crank the motor up front to start the engine. When the weather was hot, all of the windows on the auto were open. When the weather was cold or rainy, we had to put the curtains on over the windows.

I can remember when my daddy put gas in the tank under the front seat. The auto's headlights were supplied with electrical current from the generator. The faster the motor ran, the brighter the lights burned.

Heating and cooling played another major role in our lives. We never heard of an air-conditioner. During the hot weather, we opened the windows to the house so a nice breeze would go through. At night, I can remember lying up in the open window with my face right against the window screen to try and get a cool breeze.

Of course, for those who were imaginative, inventive, and really ingenious, the problem could be solved. We had a neighbor who rigged up a small platform in the tree outside of his bedroom window. He placed a block of ice on the platform. Then, he ran an extension cord to his electric fan which he sat behind the block of ice. All night he had real cool air blowing into his bedroom window,

All of my young life, when the weather got cold, my family stayed warm by shoveling coal into the furnace down in the basement. Also, in the early mornings, we burned coal in the grate in the living room.

In the winter, I can remember getting up every morning to get ready to go to school. I would get out of bed and run like crazy through the cold house to get to the grate in the living room where I could stand by the burning hot coals and get dressed. I always turned on the radio, or I put an old 78 RPM record on the wind-up Victrola so I could listen to music while I was getting dressed.

Today, all we have to do is touch a button on the thermostat in the house to turn on either the heat or the air-conditioning.

Some people might say, "Wow, you really had it rough back in those old days!"

I would say, "I don't know... I got to hear a lot of good music on the radio and records while I dressed in front of the warm grate in the living room. And, I didn't even have to punch any buttons!"

Along the Scouting Trail

Do you remember the old Burk & Company building on Church Street between Fourth and Fifth Avenues? At one time, Shacklett's Cafeteria was across the street from Burk's before moving to the corner of Fifth and Church on the first floor of the Jackson Building. Cain-Sloan Company later built at that corner having moved from across the street when Harvey's expanded over the full block. Now, are you totally confused? Today, regrettably, Burk's, Shacklett's, Cain-Sloan, and Harvey's are all gone.

To early Nashvillians, that old Burk & Company building was the Masonic Hall and Theatre. However, that was before my time. In 1913, the location was occupied by Burk & Company. Much later it became Gus Mayer's department store.

Burk & Company was important to me when I was growing up, because that is where my parents took me to buy my Boy Scout uniform and equipment including my Boy Scout Handbook.

As I now sit at my computer in my office, I am only about ten feet away from my book shelves where my first Boy Scout Handbook sits. That book is now close to three-quarters of a century old. I treasure every aging page within that archaic binding.

On that memorable day at Burk & Company, when I was so excited in the anticipation of buying my Scout uniform, I remember that we were in line behind a couple of policemen and a fireman who were there to purchase their uniforms, also. At that time, Burk's was the distributor of their uniforms as well as the Boy Scout uniforms.

Over the years, I remember that scouts attended handicraft workshops at Burk's. I remember doing some leather craft work there on Saturday mornings. We worked at tables up on the mezzanine floor. I remember two scout leaders who helped a lot at those workshops. They were Charles Mott and Scobey Rogers, Jr.

Scobey and his parents became wonderful friends over the years. My sister and I used to go to their home to play badminton and other games. Scobey's mother and father always were anxious to help and sponsor the work of the Boy Scouts.

I remember that Mr. Scobey Rogers, Sr. was the treasurer of Standard Candy Company. And, what did we get for Christmas each year? Certainly. One of those great tins of peppermint stick candy that only Standard Candy Company could make in their special way. Standard also made Goo Goo candy bars.

I am afraid too many of my old Scout buddies at Troop 26 are now gone. But, once in a while I hear from Hi Brown, and run across several like James Kilgore and Tom Fisher. When we talk, we don't have to explain anything to each other, because our memories are bulging with the same thoughts and feelings and joys that each of us experienced.

Boy Scout Troop 26 (the Service Troop) was sponsored by old Waverly Place Methodist Church which was located at the corner of Tenth Avenue, South and Caruthers Avenue. That church congregation has long since moved to a different location. Even the name of the church has changed. Old Waverly Place is now Forest Hills United Methodist Church on Old Hickory Boulevard near Brentwood.

Our scout troop met every Friday night in the scout cabin which we built ourselves. The cabin was located in the then wooded triangular area where Ninth Avenue, South intersects with Vaulx Lane.

Our scoutmaster was Mr. William L. Northern. I remember some of us going over to his home many times to practice sending and receiving Morse Code. Mr. Northern bought an electronic code sender on which we could practice Morse Code since many of us at the time were interested in becoming ham radio operators.

Bill Northern, his son, was older than I, but I knew him well. Billy was killed while flying a patrol mission off our northwest coast right before hostilities actually began for us in World War II.

If you are ever in Tullahoma, Tennessee, look at the name of the air field there. It is Northern Field named in memory of Billy Northern.

Paul Hughes was an assistant scoutmaster of troop 26. I saw Paul just a few years ago at one of the Hume-Fogg High School reunions held at the Hermitage Hotel. Paul passed away soon after that.

James Kilgore was an active leader in our troop 26. My wife, my sister, and I attended his 80th birthday open house a while back given by his daughter. Also, I have had the pleasure of being with him several times when we visit Forest Hills United Methodist Church.

James Kilgore has always been interested in photography, both still shots and moving pictures. Back in our scouting days, James produced a movie film titled *Along the Scouting Trail.* Many of us scouts were in the picture, and the production was well done.

Many of us attended the scouts' annual field days held at Dudley Field. Also, scouts ushered at all of the Vanderbilt home football games.

Our troop would be invited out to Happy Valley Farm owned by a Mr. Gant. His farm was located just off of Franklin Pike a little bit south of the WSM radio tower.

At Happy Valley Farm we cooked our own food, we used the cold spring as our icebox, we slept in the hay loft of the barn, and we experienced the pure air and wide open spaces as we were taught many things that would help us through life.

All of us scouts attended old Camp Boxwell located on our scenic Harpeth River off of Highway 70 near the Harpeth Narrows. Let me tell you about some of the sun-bleached driftwood of my memory.

One day, I drove my family down the road to where the old Camp Boxwell was located.

The old, walking, swinging bridge across the river is gone. Near that spot today, there is a paved road across a new bridge. The hillside where all of the tents were set up for camp has grown over with weeds. Weeds have also taken over the areas where the mess hall stood, and where our reveilles were held out around the flag pole.

I could see where the swimming dock used to be on the river bank. The river looks the same.

Upstream the tunnel that Montgomery Bell dug through the hillside which connected two parts of the river called The Narrows is still there.

What was missing were the sounds, joyous yelling and talk between scouts as we paddled our canoes through that part of life which was teaching us as we struggled how to become men.

Our scout troop was dissolved many years ago, but the old cabin we built has been renovated, and it is now the home of the Mount Parah Primitive Baptist Church. I am pleased that the old building still stands and is being used.

Fourteen Miles, My Foot!

Back in the 1930s, during the New Deal of the administration of President Franklin D. Roosevelt, we were inundated with many acronyms such as PWA, CWA, NRA, CCC, and WPA among others.

During the years we were pulling out of The Great Depression, Nashville prospered from many federal grants by the WPA (Works Progress Administration) which was developed by President Roosevelt and the New Deal.

Nashville received federal money to build our airport. The WPA was administered in Tennessee by Colonel Harry S. Berry. When Nashville got the much needed new airport through help from this program, it was named Berry Field in honor of Colonel Berry.

Also, through help from this program we received a state supreme court building, some other state office buildings, a new post office on Broadway which is now the Frist Center for the Visual Arts, and a new courthouse.

The courthouse was dedicated in 1937. It was built at the same site on the Public Square as was each of the other buildings which date back to the 1780s.

This federal program also provided funds for some construction and improvements in Percy Warner Park and Edwin Warner Park.

As we drive on Old Hickory Boulevard after turning off of Highway 100, Percy Warner Park is on the left side of the road, and Edwin Warner Park is on the right side of Old Hickory Boulevard.

The parks were given as gifts from Percy Warner's son-in-law, Luke Lea, also from Percy's brother Edwin, as well as some other sources I understand. Back then, Percy Warner was the chairman of the city's park board.

If you don't remember Luke Lea, he began the publication of the *Nashville Tennessean* newspaper, which was a prohibition newspaper. Later, Luke Lea was a World War I hero, and served as a senator from Tennessee.

Percy Warner Park is made up of about 2,050 acres. Edwin Warner Park is smaller and is approximately 607 acres. The parks are operated under the jurisdiction of the Metropolitan Board of Parks and Recreation.

When I was a child, I remember some great times out in the parks. There were roads for autos to travel, trails for walkers, and trails for horseback riding. There used to be some nice horse stables in Edwin Warner Park near the golf course as you head up toward Cheekwood today.

I remember strict rules in the parks. We were told not to get off of the hiking trails. We were diligent in protecting the plants, animals, rocks, and minerals.

I remember as a young Boy Scout, we had a requirement to do a 14-mile hike. So, one Saturday morning, our patrol leader, Billy Wright, of the Cobra patrol of old Troop 26, had us hike from our homes in Belmont Heights to the entrance of Percy Warner Park which we still can see at the end of Belle Meade Boulevard.

When our patrol leader said we had walked fourteen miles, I laughed and said, "Fourteen miles, my foot!" Personally, I think the trip was over 20 miles since we walked all over the park, too. But, we did it and we had a wonderful time soaking up the nature of the beautiful park.

The Nature Center in the parks was a place worth enjoying, but it was small. Even bad weather would cancel certain events. But, now there is a newer Learning Center off of Highway 100 on the Edwin Warner Park side.

This new Susanne Warner Bass Learning Center is named in honor of Edwin Warner's youngest daughter Susanne, in appreciation of her support of the construction of this Learning Center.

Sorrowfully, Susanne Warner Bass passed away on Sunday, May 14, 2000, at the age of 90.

The farmhouse that is the library building is named for daughter Milbrey Warner Waller, and the cabin serving as the administration building is named for daughter Emily Warner Dean.

Thanks to the great parks, we Nashvillians can still enjoy and live amidst Mother Nature.

I shall always remember my first real acquaintance with the park even if my feet hurt. I enjoyed walking to and all around the park when I was about thirteen years old.

Fourteen miles, my foot!

Can You Sing "Y M C A ?"

The year was 1939. I was fifteen years old. I had the opportunity to become a member of the YMCA. At the tail-end of The Great Depression, I really didn't know much about the YMCA. At that time, I was very interested in the Boy Scouts, advancing up to Eagle Scout, and going to old Camp Boxwell on the Harpeth River located near The Narrows of the Montgomery Bell family fame.

At that time, the YMCA building was located downtown at the southeast corner of Seventh Avenue, North and Union Street. Later, the building was torn down and the Hyatt Regency Hotel went up on that corner. The hotel has gone through a number of different names, but there is still the hotel at that corner today.

The corner of Seventh Avenue and Union Street has changed quite a bit over the years. Back in my youth, at the northeast corner was the War Memorial Building which is still there. At the southwest corner were the old James K. Polk Apartments with a very long sidewalk leading up to the building. On the northwest corner (diagonally across from the YMCA) was the National Life & Accident Insurance Company building. The top floor of the insurance building was where WSM radio was located. I know a lot about that since I played some on the radio there as a musician.

One day in this year of 1939, I learned that the YMCA had a band, and everyone who played in the band on Saturday mornings was given a free YMCA membership for Saturdays.

I looked into the matter, and to my great amazement, I learned that the director of the band was none other than Mr. Jack Kendall who owned the music store where my parents had bought my first clarinet.

At that time, Kendall's Nashville Band Instrument Company was located on upper Eighth Avenue across and above where the old Tulane Hotel used to stand at the corner of Eighth Avenue and Church Street. Across Church Street from the Tulane Hotel was the Paramount Theatre. Of course, this was before streets were changed to accommodate James Robert Parkway and the surrounding area.

When I approached Mr. Kendall, he said, "You bet your life you can play in the band, and I will turn your name in for your YMCA membership for Saturdays."

On Saturday mornings, the band rehearsals were very enjoyable, and Mr. Kendall taught us a great deal.

After we finished the rehearsal, the entire band was free to stay at the YMCA and participate in everything. We played basketball, volleyball, ping pong, lifted weights, and did other activities. I always enjoyed running on the track which was way up near the ceiling above a gymnasium.

Finally, a whistle blew, and all of us got ready to go into the indoor swimming pool. Of course, all of the members were boys back then. The girls had their own YWCA program which was located across the street on Seventh

Avenue, North, a few doors up from the old Doctors Building and the Bennie Dillon Building.

The old YMCA building was built in 1912, some 27 years before I entered its hallowed halls. It was eight stories tall. It included dormitories, four gymnasiums, an indoor swimming pool, offices, and classrooms. A law school was established there. The old Nashville Business College was housed there, also.

Around 1921 following World War I, the YMCA found itself in serious debt. Mr. H. G. Hill became the president of the YMCA; and, with his financial know-how, lifted the Y from its debts through The Great Depression. It is told that during some of those years, Mr. Horace G. Hill actually helped the YMCA make its payroll and keep it going.

During World War II of the 1940s, the structure was almost entirely turned over to the U. S. O. (United Service Organization.)

In the 1950s, Horace G. Hill, Jr. became president of the YMCA. The programs and activities were enlarged. Mr. Hill fostered the Youth in Government program.

Beginning in the 1960s, the East Y and other expansions began to come into being. In 1966, Mr. H. G. Hill, Jr. gave 8.5 acres of land on Hillsboro Circle to establish what is now the Green Hills Family YMCA. My wife and I are members there. We participate in the KeenAgers strength training program for seniors. Someday we hope to transfer our membership to a new Bellevue Family YMCA.

In 1969, the Y again expanded its programs, and began its inner-city outreach work. A new YMCA location was built in Donelson-Hermitage, and the Downtown and Northwest centers were built. Soon, the Harding Place,

Franklin, Rutherford County, Brentwood, Maury County, Robertson County, Madison and other facilities were opened. If one is a member of any center, the membership can be used at all YMCAs throughout the entire country.

Sonia and I became charter members of the Maury County Family YMCA in Columbia, TN when our son-in-law, Jeffery D. Parsley, was sent as the executive director to build it. We watched it as it was being built. We saw that Y go from a vacant lot to a thriving Family YMCA facility.

In 2001, the Middle Tennessee YMCA celebrated 125 years of its existence. The Y now sees such programs and activities as before-and-after-school child care, nurseries, Kids Clubs, teen centers, leadership groups, senior's health programs, aquatics for all ages, gymnastics, weight rooms, health and wellness centers, and much more.

Today, the YMCA centers are open to everyone including all members of the family, and people of all faiths. That is why we now call it the Family YMCA.

We are thankful for this institution in our communities which stresses the need for good family life, the training of our youth, and health benefits for all people.

Mayor Ben West at Union Station, 1962

Nashville's Life Keeps Changing

We reach across the years to rouse emotions of nostalgia.

Steam engine

E.D. Thompson during World War II c. 1940s

Old Schools Encase Many Memories

Do you remember some of the old schools for Nashvillians such as Wallace Academy, Morgan Prep School, Duncan School, Webb School, Tarbox, Central High School, Isaac Litton High, Columbia Military Academy, Castle Heights Military Academy, North High School, Howard High School, Pearl High School, Haynes High School, Cameron High School, and Peabody Demonstration School, to name a few?

There were many old Davidson County Schools and Nashville City Schools. We used to have two separate school systems headed by two different school superintendents and two different school boards.

Some time back, there were rumblings of the possibility of destroying the old Eakin and Cavert School buildings on Fairfax Avenue. My eyes and ears perked up with great interest at the mention of those schools.

I attended Clemons School on 12th Avenue, South when I was an elementary school student. I am proud to say that the former students of Clemons hold a reunion every five years. The last reunion was at the new and beautiful Richland Country Club off of Granny White Pike.

I recognized many old friends, but it was remarkable how all of them seemed to have gotten so much older than I!

Our Clemons School was torn down many years ago. The remnants of the old concrete steps which led up to the school building still remain by the sidewalk on 12th Avenue, South between Linden and Ashwood Avenues.

Back in those days, we had elementary schools, junior high schools, and high schools. The 9th grade, which was really the freshman year of high school, was in the junior high school building. High schools were for 10th, 11th, and 12th grades only.

When Waverly-Belmont Junior High School was built around 1936 at the corner of Tenth Avenue, South and Caruthers Avenue, my class was the first to go into the new junior high building.

I have great remembrances of Cavert Junior High School, because Waverly-Belmont and Cavert played each other in sports, and we were great rivals.

Thankfully, the students, teachers, parents, community members, and Historic Nashville, Inc. fought a good fight to arrive at a positive outcome for the fate of Eakin and Cavert schools.

Finally, the Metro Council passed an ordinance to place an Historic Landmark District designation on the Eakin and Cavert buildings.

Other great schools have been preserved in Nashville. My sister graduated from Hume-Fogg High School, and I attended there for my sophomore year of high school. Around 1940, when Hume-Fogg was to become a technical and vocational high school, I transferred to the newer West End High School located at West End and Bowling Avenues. I am thankful and proud to have been a part of Hume-Fogg, even if it were just for one year.

Another wonderful building used to house the students at Fall School located at the corner of Eighth Avenue, South and Chestnut Street near Greer Stadium.

Fall School was built in 1898, and was used by our Board of Education until the 1970s. My sister's sister-in-law by the name of Sara Griffin taught at that school, and we know something of its greatness in educational achievements.

The old Fall School structure was built with a 60-feet high atrium skylight, and an atrium fountain. These were unusual features for a school building back in 1898.

In the 1980s, Eric Ericson bought the building and began an extensive renovation for his large advertising and marketing firm.

Now, the great old building has become the Fall School Business Center with many business offices located there.

Back in the 1960s, the public school system found no need for an elementary school in that Fall School area. So, students at Fall School merged with Hamilton School creating the Fall-Hamilton School which is located at 510 Wedgewood Avenue near the Fairgrounds.

Back around 1971, I was privileged to work at Fall-Hamilton School on an educational project while I served on the faculty of Belmont College. So, I can proudly say that I had at least a small role in working in the changing process of old Fall School.

Some of our schools are things of the past, but still live in many of our memories.

One of our great old institutions was Tarbox School built in 1886 as part of the old Nashville City School System. The school was torn down in the 1960s. It was a red brick, rather odd looking structure, on Broad Street near Division.

The first principal of Tarbox was Professor George Elliot. Several of that school's early teachers had other schools named for them. For instance, there was Mr. John E. Bailey (my wife attended Bailey School in East Nashville), Mr. A. M. Cavert, and Mrs. Emma Clemons had schools named for them.

If you went to a city public school back in those days, then you remember Mr. Milton Cook who came around to each school periodically and taught us music. Also, Miss Cornelius came to our schools at certain times to teach us art.

Burton School, a Davidson County elementary school, sat for many years on Granny White Pike. Today, the old Burton School has been beautifully remodeled including additions, and it is now the David Lipscomb Elementary School.

Palmer School was a wonderful school under the efficient leadership of Miss Lucille Talley, the principal. The old school is gone, but often I drive on Leake Avenue between Harding Road and Belle Meade Boulevard, and at least can still see the front entrance of the school standing proudly as a monument to the old elementary school. The area behind that old brick and stone entrance is now a nice park area and playground.

Woodmont School, another Davidson County elementary school, once located on Estes Road off of Woodmont Boulevard at Woodmont Circle is no longer there. Today, that area is called Woodmont Park. It includes a tennis court, basketball court, a playground, and picnic tables.

In years gone by, we had TIS which stood for Tennessee Industrial School. Later, that school which was located on Foster Avenue off of Murfreesboro Road was renamed TPS which stood for Tennessee Preparatory School.

Do many of you old high school students remember taking manual training or industrial arts, home economics, typing, or Gregg shorthand?

During the 1940s, I graduated from West End High School, and my wife, Sonia, graduated from East Nashville High School. There is something interesting about the towers at each school building.

West End High, home of the Blue Jays, was the last high school built with a bell tower. The bell came from the Buena Vista Grammar School in North Nashville.

During the 1946-47 school year at East High, home of the Eagles, a clock was placed in the school tower in memory of the 59 Armed Forces service people from East High who lost their lives in World War II. Purposely, the circumference of the clock was made 59 inches, representing one inch for each service person who died.

There really are a lot of things worth remembering!

Ushering in the Forties

My father died when I was sixteen years old. In that year of 1941, I was a junior in West End High School in Nashville.

When my school let out for the summer, I hit the sidewalks to try and find a job. I admittedly was the worst possible person to go in places and ask for a job.

I told my mother, "I found out that a shoe store downtown is hiring some of my friends on weekends."

So, I put on my nice clothes and went downtown in search of a job.

I got off the streetcar and walked down Church Street. I passed where we used to see great vaudeville acts at the Princess Theatre. My father especially liked a harmonica player by the name of Brentwood who often appeared on the Princess stage shows.

I turned north on Fifth Avenue. I always enjoyed walking past the Rex Theatre and the Fifth Avenue Theatre so I could look at the show cards to see what was playing. When I got to the Arcade, I crossed the street over to the shoe store. All the way, I was practicing what I would say to the store manager.

I timidly walked into the store and asked to speak to the manager. When the tall and blusterous store manager walked up, even before I could finish my first sentence, this shoe store manager said that he had nothing for me.

This youthful lad of sixteen couldn't even talk a story-line well enough to seek a job. Also, I gave the appearance of the world's worst shoe salesman.

I, being the type person that would not give up too quickly at anything, had another brain-storm. I decided that I might want to be an usher at a movie theatre. That sounded glamorous to me. The movie house ushers wore uniforms. They got to see all of the movies free, too.

The next day in my search for a job during the summer of 1941, I took the Belmont Heights streetcar to downtown Nashville and went in Loew's Vendome Theatre on Church Street at the foot of Capitol Boulevard. I got excited as I walked into the lobby.

When my wife, I, and our friends came up in the thirties and forties, movie theatres were a different thing from what they are today. Back then, the Paramount, Knickerbocker, Princess, Loew's, and every theatre needed ushers.

Theatres were beautiful and spacious. The beauty and ornateness of many theatres took on an attitude of the Renaissance, Baroque, Rococo, Classic, Gothic, Moorish, or some other exotic architecture.

There were large canopies over the theatre entrances, and well-lighted marquees were frantically busy with colorful chaser light bulbs.

One would walk into impressive and spacious lobbies. In addition, there were vestibules, foyers, lounges, waiting rooms, and promenades. There were marble statuary, and plush stairways to mezzanines and balconies. A plush and velvet environment permeated the entire scene.

In those days, the theatres were packed for every showing. The patrons expected to see a feature film, or maybe a double feature. In addition, we were treated to short subjects like a travelogue, Robert Benchley or Pete Smith specials. That's not all. Surely there would be a cartoon, on some days an adventure serial, and a short newsreel.

We used to be able to enter a movie at any time during the showing. We would stay until where we came in and then we would leave, unless we wanted to stay through the picture again. That's where the expression, "This is where I came in," came from.

Very few people came in the theatre right at the beginning of the picture. No one had to. The plots of many movies weren't extremely involved. You could catch up on what was happening on most of them. There were a lot of song and dance and big Hollywood production numbers.

Since I loved the movies, I got the idea to apply for an usher's job. I saw those ushers neatly dressed in their dark trousers with a stripe down the side, their white shirts, black ties, white gloves, and short vests lined with about six bright buttons. Ushers were needed in those days. They would shine their flashlight on the floor while they took a patron over the plush carpet to a vacant seat.

On that day of job hunting, I entered the theatre with high expectations of landing a job. I walked up to one of the ushers in the theatre (of all people) and asked if they needed another usher. Of course, the usher said "No." If there had been an opening, that usher would have told one of his friends about it, not me!

I later realized that I should have gone to see the manager to inquire about a vacancy. I reflected, "How stupid could I have been?"

Finally, on that day, I took the Belmont streetcar back home feeling somewhat dejected to say the least. I had to figure out a different plan of attack on getting a job.

Church Street looking East

Remembering Radio WLAC (circa 1940s)

At the age of sixteen, following the death of my father in 1941, the Golden Age of Radio came into my life.

I played an accordion before I engaged in formal study of clarinet and saxophone, and before I performed professionally on those instruments. Elva, my big sister, was working during 1937 at Cumberland Manufacturing Company down near the hay market between Third and Fourth Avenues. I was twelve years old, and she bought and gave me my first accordion.

I tried to get a job at a shoe store, but I couldn't. I tried to get a job of ushering in a theatre, but I couldn't.

A few days later that summer of 1941, while feeling dejected over not locating some employment, I received a telephone call from my old accordion teacher, Mr. Fred Murff. He taught accordion lessons at Claude P. Street Piano Company on Church Street across the alley near the Paramount Theatre.

"Hello. Yes, Mr. Murff. It is good to hear your voice."

"E. D., you told me that you were interested in locating a job this summer, right?"

I quickly responded, "Yes sir, I am."

"Well, I learned that radio station WLAC is looking for an accordion player for a new morning program. You may want to give the station a call."

After much excitement in thanking my old teacher, I grabbed the telephone book, looked up the number and called the radio station. My call got an appointment to meet with the fellow in charge of developing the new morning program.

Radio in the forties was everything in the lives of people. Whole families listened to many wonderful programs during the Golden Age of Radio.

Old radio shows with drama, music, romance, and mystery were great because they made us use our imagination. Family members listening together couldn't see the action, but our minds listened and painted pictures.

When I got to WLAC for my appointment, I met the fellow in charge of developing the new morning program. He was Paul Oliphant. I had heard him on the air many times. Now, I was seeing him face to face.

Paul Oliphant was one of the station's top announcers. Every Saturday morning, Paul was the announcer on a garden show called *The Garden Gate*. Paul, along with the gardening man known as "The Old Dirt Dobber," was fed to the CBS radio network from Nashville.

Paul, in addition to his announcing talent, was a guitar player and a good singer. The new morning show Paul was to develop would be called *Ranch House Melodies*, a fifteen-minute country and western musical show.

I followed Paul Oliphant back into the studios of WLAC for my audition. The radio station took up the entire top floor of the then Third National Bank Building located at the corner of Fourth Avenue, North and Church Street. This building was diagonally across the street from the old Maxwell House Hotel which was at Fourth and Church. This old bank building preceded the new Third National Bank Building which later was built on the site of the old Maxwell House Hotel after the hotel burned.

WLAC radio had three studios in a semi-circular arrangement with a glassed-in control room in the middle area so the engineers could see in all three studios.

WLAC's studio B was quite large compared to today's standard. Studio C in the middle was where the announcers worked. And, Studio A was a large performance studio. In Studio A, the station's studio orchestra, which was conducted by the fine violinist, Charles Nagy, stayed set up on risers with drums, piano, music stands, and everything for use at all times.

Also, Studio A had a pipe organ installed. In those days, you could hear an announcer say, "And now, an organ interlude with Mary Elizabeth Hicks at the console of the giant Kilgen."

The announcers at that time were Paul Oliphant, Charlie Roberts, Tim Sanders, Charles Chumley, and Herman Grizzard who also did the announcing at the old Sulphur Dell ball park where the Nashville Vols played baseball. The station manager at that time was Mr. F. C. Sowell. Mr. Truman Ward was then owner. Mr. Ward's secretary back in the forties was Bellevue's Sara Elizabeth Wilhite.

I passed the audition. After many hours of rehearsals and a prepared repertoire of one hundred songs, *Ranch House Melodies* went on the air. There were three of us. A fine mandolin player from Old Hickory was called Red. Paul assumed the name of Curly. And, I was proud to be hailed by the radio name, Shorty.

Curly, Red, and Shorty went on the air in the summer of 1941. For a time, we were playing as many as nine 15-minute programs a week. Some shows were sponsored, and some were sustaining which meant that WLAC paid us for those. Once a week, I would go down on lower Broadway to get my pay from Morris Furniture Company which sponsored some of the programs.

I was paid three dollars a show. Nine shows times three dollars was $27.00 per week. For a sixteen-year-old kid back in the early forties, that was big money!

As the threat of World War II advanced, the government demanded that all radio stations lock off their transmitting facilities. This was to prevent an enemy take over, or the possibility of sabotage to the communication systems of the country.

One morning, I found myself blocked from the studios on the top floor of the old Third National Bank Building. I was shocked to find a gate had been constructed and locked with a heavy duty lock. However, one loud shout each morning easily got me admitted to the studios by the engineer from the control room. That was the beginning of the interruptions to everyone's life due to the war.

In those days, the program following *Ranch House Melodies* was *Big Jeff and the Radio Playboys*. Big Jeff was the husband of the famous "Tootsie" Bess who owned and operated Tootsie's Orchid Lounge on Broadway. Tootsie's real name was Hattie Louise Bess.

Whenever I meet people, and they learn that I used to play at WLAC, the first words out of their mouths are, "Oh, then you knew Hoss Allen."

Then, I have to explain that Hoss Allen came to WLAC after I had worked there. Hoss Allen, truly known as a legend in radio circles, came to WLAC in 1949. I played there in 1941. But, then I have to explain, "Yes, I knew Hoss Allen, but not in the way you think!"

It was in early 1943. John Stalin was a student at Vanderbilt University and had organized a great dance orchestra. The band was playing jobs all around town.

I was a freshman music major at Peabody College, and one day I was called to take a job with the John Stalin Orchestra at the old Maxwell House Hotel. They needed a substitute saxophone player for that job. I was delighted to get to play with that wonderful 15-piece dance orchestra. I knew many of the Vanderbilt and Peabody students in the band.

That night of the job, I walked up that fabulous historic staircase in the Maxwell House Hotel where Presidents and Generals had strolled, and made my way from the lobby to the mezzanine. From there I went into the spacious ballroom, sauntered up to the bandstand, and began to get my saxophone and clarinet out of the cases.

I looked up, and I saw a student approaching, attired in his nicely pressed, tailored tuxedo, ready to step upon the bandstand. I had never seen a more dapper, well-groomed person in my life. As for me, I had to try and fit my old tuxedo around me the best I could!

Another band member introduced me to this student, "Buddy, meet Bill Allen. He is the drummer on our band."

Yes, I knew Bill "Hoss" Allen, but I knew him as a dance band drummer, and not through WLAC.

After I returned home from the Army, I got to play some more at WLAC in the live staff orchestra. Charles Nagy, who had been the orchestra leader at WLAC, had died of cancer. The orchestra after the war was led by two great friends, my old accordion teacher, Fred Murff, and one of the loveliest ladies in radio, Mary Elizabeth Hicks, who was the staff organist and pianist at WLAC radio for 28 years.

There was a time when WLAC decided to have deejays play records on the air, push their advertisers, and have a more intimate rapport with their listeners.

The national coverage of John Richburg (known on the air as John R.), Gene Nobles, and Bill "Hoss" Allen came onto the scene. WLAC's signal covered about 40 states at night.

In the 1960s, WLAC adopted a top-40 format. Then, later became a "talk radio" station.

There have always been arguments as to whom started the talk shows in Nashville. Well, as I remember, there were scattered talk shows on various stations all along the way. I remember when I was working on a graduate degree at Peabody College in the 1960s, I always ate lunch in my car out by the old tennis courts. And, I always turned on the radio to hear Roland Wolfe and his talk show over WLAC. Also, Teddy Bart had a talk show early on at WSM. And, there were others.

Many years have now passed. In 1968, J. C. Bradford Company moved into the old building at Fourth and Church for about an eighteen year stay. Then, the great old building sat empty for about eleven years, from 1986 until 1997. I was frightened that the good building would be torn down. Not so! Plans moved toward renovating the building and becoming a Courtyard by Marriott Hotel.

WLAC Radio, 1510 on your AM dial, celebrated its 75th anniversary back in 2002. I shall always cherish the great memories of the days I played in old Studio A atop the Third National Bank Building downtown at the corner of Fourth and Church.

The Arcade Still Lives Today

There is a structure in our city which many people take for granted, but a structure which was unique when it opened in 1903.

The Arcade downtown between Fourth and Fifth Avenues, North truly amazed people of that era. The Arcade celebrated its 100th anniversary in 2003.

The Arcade was built as a block-long mall housing more than 50 shops on two levels under a gabled glass roof. It was an identical copy of the Galleria Vittorio Emmanuele II arcade in Milan, Italy.

Back in the old days, the Arcade was decorated with American flags and other decorative banners hanging from the balcony. The Arcade displayed sparkling store windows, and a smooth pavement which brought a gala shopping center atmosphere to Nashvillians where ladies wore long skirts and fashionable hats when they went to town.

I remember many shops that were present there when I was young. I remember the United Jewelers, a shop called Arcade Hose, Cato's Malt Shop where we could get a cold, refreshing dessert, a shoe repair shop where we could have our shoes half-soled, and a trunk and bag company where, at one time, I bought a Christmas present for my wife.

The Peanut Shop has been there for ages. The Peanut Man used to stand out in front of the door and give away samples. And, you know what happens when you eat one peanut! You can't eat just one peanut! You have to go inside and buy a bag full. Of course, we really needed them anyway just before we headed out to the Knickerbocker, Loew's, or Paramount Theatre.

The Peanut Shop opened in 1927. In 1960, the company decided to sell the various stores around the country to individuals. The present owner of The Peanut Shop in the Arcade is Kathy Bloodworth.

The same scales that weighed nuts 75 years ago still weighs them now. The same red pot-bellied roaster used 75 years ago is still used today. The same peanut-patterned wallpaper covers the ceiling.

It seems like the post office branch has been in the Arcade forever. It has zip code 37219 for the downtown merchants.

I remember a drugstore always being on the corner of the Arcade at Fifth Avenue. A Walgreens Drugstore is there now.

Today, if you stroll down the Arcade, you will see a florist, jewelry store, and a shoe shop where you can get a shine or get your shoes repaired.

There are tables along the Arcade where you can sit and enjoy tasteful edibles from many different food shops.

You will see the Oriental Lunch, and the Arcade Fruit Stand. You can enjoy a treat from the Planet Smoothie, and a varied selection of other types of food fare.

Of all the old shops that used to be in the Arcade, one is prominent in my life. A music student since age twelve, a high school band member, and then a college music major, I spent a great deal of time shopping at Strobel's Music Shop.

The very polite and gentle Robert W. Strobel knew all of the needs of the musician, both amateur and professional. In addition to all needed instruments, sheet music supplies, and everything else for the musician, Strobel's also had an instrument repairman who had his shop on the second floor. Mr. Ralph Covey was the finest instrument repairman around at the time. There was nothing that he could not do.

I knew two of Mr. Strobel's sons. Ray worked there in the family store with his dad. Another son, Bob, was a student at Peabody College the same time I was there. Bob was an outstanding tenor. He did roles in opera performances we presented at Peabody in the summertime on the big outdoor stage in front of the Social-Religious Building.

Nashville and our Southern traditions always had people that found a way to help you out when in need? There is a memory about Mr. Strobel that I shall never forget.

It was April in the year of 1943. I, along with many others, left Nashville to serve in the U. S. Armed Forces during World War II. Our train load went from Nashville's Union Station to Chattanooga, and then by bus on over to Fort Oglethorpe, Georgia for our induction into the United States Army. Once at Fort Oglethorpe, we were processed and assigned to bases all over America. I shipped out to Camp Grant near Rockford, Illinois.

While at this camp, a dance band was formed to entertain the troops. I was fortunate enough to get to play lead alto saxophone on the band with some fine musicians who had played on big bands.

A special services officer at the camp loved dance bands, and he was the driving force behind organizing this band. When the other troops had to go on KP [kitchen police,] latrine duty, or some other undesirable detail, this officer would call a rehearsal of the band. Also, he even located an alto saxophone for me to play.

I played this GI horn for a while. Then, I decided I should call home and have my mother ship my own horn to me at camp. My mother took my saxophone downtown to Strobel's Music Shop in the Arcade. Mr. Strobel graciously packed the horn, got it to the post office, and shipped it to my address at Camp Grant, Illinois.

If you remember what "snafu" means, well it happened! My horn was on route to Camp Grant. The next day, I was shipped out to San Francisco, California. I rushed to call my mother. My mother rushed back to Mr. Strobel.

You know the rest of the story. Mr. Strobel graciously went to work to trace my saxophone package through the post office. He was successful, and my horn was returned to my home in Nashville. That was the same horn that I later played for many years in bands after returning to Nashville from the Army.

What nostalgic emotions do you think I feel when I walk down the Arcade today and pass the old location where Strobel's Music Shop used to stand?

"Neither Snow nor Rain

nor gloom of night stays these couriers from the swift completion of their appointed rounds" is the motto of our United States Postal Service.

Do you remember where Nashville's post office was before the one next to Union Station on Broadway was built? It was at Seventh and Broadway in the Customs House, a building which still stands today.

Do you remember when the mail carriers made two walking deliveries each day? Of course, they didn't walk in the rural areas. That mail delivery was called R. F. D. It stood for rural free delivery.

Do you remember when the mail carriers had a whistle attached to their jackets? If no one was outside at home, the postman would blow his whistle after he placed your mail in the mailbox to announce that the mail had been delivered.

When I was a child growing up, I remember that our postman sorted the mail each morning for his route. Then, he caught a Belmont Heights streetcar out from town to our community. With a large, heavy, leather mail bag on his shoulder, he walked his appointed rounds.

The mail carriers were friends of everyone on their routes. Each postman came up on each front porch to place the mail in the mailbox. While there, he asked about everybody, and how we were getting along.

When he finished his route, he caught a streetcar and headed back downtown to the post office. Sometimes a mail truck would take the recently received mail out to a green mail storage box in the communities. The postman would unlock the box with his key, and put the new mail in his delivery bag. He once again went to his assigned community, and walked his afternoon route delivering the mail from his large, heavy, leather, shoulder mailbag.

During World War II, while I was in the Army as well as others on our block, our postman, Mr. Fuller, was aware of every person in the service. Our families each day anxiously awaited the mail deliveries to see if there might be a letter from us.

Let me tell you a personal experience. On one occasion when my mother was hoping to receive a letter from me, Mr. Fuller delivered his morning route, and there was no letter from me. Mr. Fuller said, "Mrs. Thompson, I will check when I go back to town. If a letter for you has come in, I can bring it out on my afternoon delivery."

Mr. Fuller caught the Belmont streetcar, went out on his afternoon route, and made his deliveries. When he got to my house, he had to tell my mother that no letter had come in to the post office from me.

However, Mr. Fuller said, "After I finish my afternoon delivery, and when I get back to the post office, Mrs. Thompson, if a letter has come in for you, I will send it out special delivery."

Sure enough, my mother told me that late that evening, a car drove up in front of our house. A post office employee delivered a letter from me to my mother. Mr. Fuller had put a special delivery stamp on the letter paid out of his own pocket, and had the letter sent out.

I am proud of our city which is growing and becoming so important to our nation's development. But, sometimes I can't help but long for that old Nashville which wasn't so terribly large. The postman could walk up on your front porch, deliver your mail, maybe have a nice glass of iced tea, and inquire as to how everybody was getting along.

I still love my Nashville even if it is getting larger. But, there is one thing for sure which Nashville needs today. We need a lot more Mr. Fullers.

Nashville During the War Years

Sixty years ago seem such a short span of time in my thinking back over my life. That was an era in which patriotism and unity of Americanism existed. Today, we must offer constant prayers for our country and, in fact, the world.

Thinking back to the years of World War II, probably the first sign of the war era came to Nashville when Aviation Manufacturing Corporation of California (later to be called AVCO) announced plans to locate a large airplane manufacturing plant here.

The company was named Vultee Aircraft and sat adjacent to Nashville's old Berry Field. Large defense contracts poured into the Vultee plant to produce the Vultee Vengeance bombers, and the Lockheed P-38 Lightning fighters. Women streamed into Vultee, and "Rosie the riveter" became a popular symbol of women's valor.

During World War II, Nashville organized on the home front. U. S. Bonds were bought by many citizens. Bands and other entertainers developed shows to help sell bonds. I can recall when a performance ended, the master-of-ceremonies dismissed the audience by saying, "Bye Bye, Buy Bonds!"

A Tennessean who played a very active role as a statesman in our country was Cordell Hull. He served our country well as Secretary of State from 1933 to 1944 under President Franklin D. Roosevelt. Before becoming Secretary of State, Cordell Hull was a United States senator from Tennessee.

Nashville businesses played a big role in the war effort. Vultee built airplanes, and parachutes were supplied by DuPont's synthetic fibers. The Nashville Bridge Company began to build minesweepers for the Navy, combat boots were supplied by Genesco (General Shoe Corporation,) and sandbags were manufactured by Werthan Bag Company, just to name a few Nashville businesses.

Two major military installations came to our city. The Army Air Classification Center was built on Thompson Lane. The Center processed air recruits, and determined their future training as pilots, navigators, or bombardiers.

Thayer General Hospital was constructed off of White Bridge Road, and the hospital served 13,000 wounded soldiers during its time.

Thayer was converted to a Veterans Administration Hospital. It later relocated on 24th Avenue, South near Vanderbilt University where it is today.

The summer of 1941 saw the beginnings of Camp Campbell, an army training camp near Clarksville. Camp Forrest was in Tullahoma. Then, with the establishment of Smyrna Air Field, which later became Sewart Air Force Base, many GIs poured into the environs of Nashville.

Serving in the war effort, many volunteers in our city worked to organize wholesome entertainment and provide nice sleeping quarters for the many visiting GIs.

Nashville had many movie theatres, and the old Hippodrome arena on West End Avenue, where the Holiday Inn Select Vanderbilt now stands, was a highlight of local entertainment. There was a restaurant on Church Street between Seventh and Eighth Avenues called "The Mecca." Great numbers of service personnel passed through that old restaurant.

The First Presbyterian Church at Fifth and Church converted its basement to a dormitory. The YMCA, YWCA, YMHA, and YWHA offered lounges for visiting service personnel. Many citizens opened their homes to accommodate the needs of the service men and women.

When Joe Werthan of Nashville's Werthan Bag Company saw young soldiers in Centennial Park exposed to the cold one night in December of 1942, Joe decided to convert two old mansions on Elliston Place into the Werthan Service Men's Center. He offered free dormitory space to thousands of service men.

Those two old mansions were on Elliston Place in the block area where the old Father Ryan High School used to stand. All of those structures have been demolished, and are now a thing of Nashville's past, but still nostalgic to us old-timers.

Let's honor the many families who saw loved ones serve to protect our freedom then, and let's honor the men, women, and families who are serving and supporting our country today to defend freedom.

Step on a Crack, Break Your Mother's Back

Today, we are God fearing people who realize that old superstitions are not real, right, or realistic. But, it is fun to think back on all of the old quirks of tradition that have survived through the years. There are hundreds of them.

Do you remember that people used to say that if you broke a mirror, you would have seven years of bad luck? It was bad if a picture fell off the wall. Of course, you wouldn't want to walk under a ladder. As a matter of fact, for a long time, I made a definite purpose of walking under ladders if any were in my path. I just felt the urge to prove that superstitions are wrong.

Have you ever heard that you should not accept a salt shaker from the hands of another person? To keep from having bad luck, you would have to sit the salt shaker down beside the person, and let him or her pick it up. How silly!

Everybody has heard the one about a black cat running in front of your path. After seeing a black cat, I have seen many people back up, turn their car around in a driveway, and drive around the block. Now, anyone doing that foolish thing would have to use extra gas and could easily run the risk of having an accident.

Years ago I wore a hat. I learned from several people not to lay my hat on the bed. I did that once, and everybody screamed, "Don't lay your hat on the bed. It is bad luck!"

Country folk believed that it was bad luck to kill a cricket. We knew not to count the cars in a funeral procession. We knew not to walk with one shoe on and one shoe off. That was bad luck!

People would never sew something on your clothing while you were wearing it. If you needed a button sewed on your coat, you would certainly have to take off your coat before the button could be sewed on.

It was unlucky if two people while together walked around opposite sides of a post. Everyone said that it was bad luck for the bride to see the groom on their wedding day before their wedding ceremony.

We knew not to raise an umbrella in the house. People who received umbrellas for Christmas had to run outside to see how to work it.

We have heard that the number 13 is unlucky. And, of course, on Friday the 13th, people wanted to stay in bed. Personally, I can recall a lot of nice things that have happened to me on Friday the 13th.

It was considered bad luck if the first person to enter your house on the first day of January was a female. It had to be a male to enter your door on the first day of the new year.

And, step on a crack, break your mother's back!

And then, we must not overlook some of the traditional quirks of having good luck!

People nailed horseshoes over the door in their home and over the door to the barn. Good luck! You could carry a rabbit's foot in your pocket. Many people carried a buckeye. Good luck!

If you found a penny, it was considered good luck. You could wish upon a star. One could knock on wood. I have seen people take a little salt in their hand and throw it over their right shoulder. Good luck!

Brides were caught up in tradition. The person who caught the bride's bouquet was thought to be the next one to get married. And, the bride wore at her wedding something old, something new, something borrowed, and something blue.

Four-leaf clovers were considered to be good luck charms. My mother was a Christian woman and didn't believe in superstitions. However, she liked to pick four-leaf clovers. She could stand up on the porch and see four-leaf clovers on the ground. I could get down on my hands and knees and couldn't find one.

When I was in the Army during World War II, my mother enclosed a beautiful four-leaf clover in one of her letters. That in itself is not unusual. But, what is unusual is that today I still carry that four-leaf clover in my billfold. I wrapped it in wax paper. I am sure if I unwrapped it today, it would fall apart in one brittle mess.

Today, that single four-leaf clover in my billfold is more than sixty years old. It's not a superstition for good luck. It is a memory. Actually, I don't believe in luck anyway. I believe in God's blessings.

It Was Showtime in Downtown Nashville

When I was growing up in Nashville, there were six movie theatres in the downtown shopping area near Church Street. These do not include the Orpheum Theatre which I have heard about, but was before my time of going to theatres, or the Strand Theatre on Fifth Avenue which was before my time, too. Neither do they include the Crescent Theatre on Church Street between Fourth and Fifth Avenues, and the Tennessee Theatre on Church Street beside the McKendree United Methodist Church, as these theatres came along after I had grown up.

There were six downtown theatres of my childhood which still hold many nostalgic memories.

Going east on Church Street from Eighth Avenue, the first theatre was the Paramount Theatre. My childhood memories of the Paramount are of the Popeye Club on Saturday mornings. We could ride the streetcar to town for a nickel, and get in the theatre for a dime. We were entertained by stage acts, there were contests, some prizes were given, and then we enjoyed the movies.

I remember the organ rising from below the stage level. We sang songs accompanied by the organist. The screen showed the words of the songs with a bouncing ball telling us when to sing each word or syllable.

Moving east on Church Street, we came to the Loew's Vendome Theatre which sat at the foot of Capitol Boulevard. After the theatre was torn down, that area later became the Church Street Center. Now, that structure has been torn down also to make way for the new Nashville Public Library.

The Loew's Theatre had the old box seats on both sides of the auditorium remaining from the days when live plays were presented on stage.

During my time, I saw many movies at the Loew's. I especially remember all of the Andy Hardy movies starring Mickey Rooney, Lewis Stone, Fay Holden, and others like Judy Garland and Ann Rutherford.

And, of course, in 1939 Loew's was the theatre where I saw *Gone with the Wind*. It was the first movie I knew of that had an intermission in the middle of the picture.

Just up Capitol Boulevard off of Church Street was the Knickerbocker Theatre. That elongated theatre stretched between Capitol Boulevard and Sixth Avenue. There was a box office and entrance at both streets.

I saw *Kitty Foyle* there starring Ginger Rogers. Also, being a big band enthusiast, I remember seeing the film *You'll Find Out* which featured Kay Kyser and His Orchestra. The film included a portion of one of the old radio shows called *Kay Kyser's Kollege of Musical Knowledge* which I listened to regularly on the radio.

On Church Street between Fifth and Sixth Avenues was the Princess Theatre. That theatre held onto old vaudeville stage shows the longest in that area.

As a child I enjoyed hearing the pit orchestra play. I didn't realize that many years later my son, Jeff, and I would be playing in the American Legion Post 5 Band with some of those old-timers. I wish they were still around so I could ask them some questions. I have a feeling that they were some of the musicians that played in the Princess Theatre pit orchestra.

There was Bill Scott, affectionately known as Scotty, who played trumpet, Elmer Jones played clarinet, Syd Groom played trumpet, Cy Willis was a drummer, and Walter Heckman played bass. And, at one time, Phil Harris, the famous TV star, played drums in the Princess Theatre pit orchestra.

I do know that Syd Groom was the president of the Nashville local of the musicians' union from 1920 through 1923, and Walter Heckman was the local's secretary from 1925 through 1928.

On Fifth Avenue between Church Street and the Arcade, there were two theatres just across the street from the Five & Ten Cent stores. I remember the Fifth Avenue Theatre and the Rex Theatre.

I never went to a movie at the Fifth Avenue Theatre. But, one day while my mother was shopping downtown, my father took me to the Rex Theatre, and I remember that one of pictures was a documentary about a lot of the gangsters of the day. I remember seeing John Dillinger, Pretty Boy Floyd, Machine Gun Kelly, Baby Face Nelson, and others.

The beautiful Tennessee Theatre with its large canopy and well-lighted marquee with frantically busy and colorful chaser lights was built after I returned home from the Army, and, of course, I was here to see it torn down.

On the night of the Tennessee Theatre's Grand Opening, there were Hollywood type flood lights, a parade, and some guest stars to appear. Owen Bradley and His Orchestra played a performance inside on stage that night.

I played in a band outside the theatre as the Hollywood guest stars arrived in convertibles. I remember the actors were Jon Hall who used to play *Ramar of the Jungle*, Arlene Dahl, Phyllis Kirk of TV's *The Thin Man* fame, Jack Weston, and singer Gordon McCrae.

So, I can't list the Tennessee Theatre as a movie house of my childhood. I was grown and played for its Grand Opening when it was built, and lived to see it torn down. What a waste!

Now, Picture This!

You never can tell where your picture might show up!

Some time ago, I received a telephone call from one of my good musician friends, Bill Ammonette. Bill is a trumpet player with whom I have worked many jobs. Also, he was the last owner of Hewgley's Music Shop located downtown on Commerce Street. Like many small Mom and Pop shops, the big monster companies come in and smaller companies find that they cannot survive. Hewgley's Music Shop is no more.

Bill still plays trumpet with the Establishment Orchestra, and is very active in his church choir. So, with all of us, music seems to continue in our lives .

When I answered the phone, Bill said, "We were in Louisville, Kentucky this past week. I was browsing around a bookstore while Marge [Bill's wife] was shopping."

Then, he said, "I picked up a book about Nashville politics, and opened it to a page on which I had to do a double-take. There was a picture of you!"

I said, "What?" Of course, I knew nothing about it. I almost fell over. I naturally wanted to know exactly what book it was, who wrote it, and everything about it.

Bill told me the name of the book was *The Secrets of the Hopewell Box*, and was written by James D. Squires, and published by Times Books, a division of Random House.

I couldn't imagine what it was. I told Bill I was going to head out and buy a copy of the book.

I went into Bookstar bookstore in the old Belle Meade Theatre building on Harding Road. I didn't have to look too long for the book. There was a big stack of them on display right up at the front of the store.

Sure enough! I flipped through the pages, and on a photo page opposite page 150 in the book, there is a picture of Garner Robinson, after being elected sheriff in 1946, speaking into a microphone at the old Colemere Country Club on Murfreesboro Road. Behind him in the picture can be seen three of us musicians playing in the band that night. In addition to me (in my youth of 1946) sitting there holding my saxophone, there were Billy Sims, a trumpet player, and Anita Kerr sitting at the piano.

What a pleasant surprise to see my picture in such an important book. Jim Squires began his newspaper career at *The Tennessean* in 1962. Then, he served as Washington bureau chief for the *Chicago Tribune*, and later as the editor of the *Orlando Sentinel*. He and his wife now live in Versailles, Kentucky.

If you are interested in Nashville nostalgia, and Nashville politics of by-gone days, you will enjoy reading this book.

On the back cover of the book, Senator Fred Thompson endorses the book by stating,

"Jim Squires has told a uniquely hilarious yet moving story of the rough-and-tumble world of politics a generation ago...

It sure looks like politics used to be a lot more fun."

The book goes way back in Nashville history and mentions just about every person that was ever in politics here. When I read the book, I came across old Nashville names which I haven't thought about in years.

My eyes popped open and my mind got a flash of nostalgia when I saw such names as Sam Davis Bell, Lynn Bomar, Hilary Howse, Estes Kefauver, Elkin Garfinkle, Gordon Browning, Joseph W. Byrns, Ed Crump, Joe Hatcher, Z. Alexander Looby, Bill Brock, J. Carlton Loser, Prentice Cooper, Jim Nance McCord, K. D. McKellar, and Walter Stokes, Jr., just to mention a few.

Those pages are chocked full of names from Nashville's past. I'm glad I worked that job at the Colemere Club that night in 1946.

Nashville Keeps
Growing and Expanding

Nashville's past was not a diminishing road,
but a huge spring meadow upon which beautiful structures
could flourish.

Nashville Symphony Orchestra, c. 1948

From "Out in the Country" to Green Hills

Nashville has been very active over the years in operating successful ventures in the business world.

Unfortunately, over the past years, we have lost such operations as the Harvey's department stores, Castner-Knott Company, Cain-Sloan Company, the *Nashville Banner*, Opryland USA theme park, and others.

But, do you remember some of the old-time companies when they began in Nashville many years ago?

How about Keith-Simmons Company, May Hosiery Mill, Beasley Sash & Door Company, Ellis Shoe Company, Petway-Reavis, Berry-Demoville Drug Company, Burk and Company, Hirschberger Clothing Store, Harley Holt Furniture Company, Joseph Frank's on Sixth Avenue, H. Brown Furniture Company, Candyland, Phillips & Buttorff, Cutters Exchange, Lebeck Brothers department store, National Life & Accident Insurance Company, Griffin Supply Company, Cumberland Manufacturing Company, Gilbert's on the Square, and many, many more which brought significant contributions to our city.

My wife and I know a little about the coal business because her father, Mr. T. C. Young, owned the Young

Coal Company back when coal was used in schools and industry as well as in homes.

Do you remember the old Alley-Cassetty Coal Company? Around 1964, Pete Alley and G. W. West merged with Fred J. Cassetty when there were just a few coal dealers left in the city. One of the largest was St. Bernard Coal Company.

Thomas L. Cummings, Jr., the son of former Nashville Mayor Thomas L. Cummings, Sr., built a tremendous electrical sign business. His first operations were in an old Air Corps gymnasium at Berry Field.

Do you know some of the signs that Cummings Incorporated has manufactured? How about Ford, Chrysler, Conoco, Kentucky Fried Chicken, Holiday Inn, and Captain D's Seafood, to name just a few.

Levy's, that well-known men's fashion store, had its beginnings about a century and a half ago when Zadoc Levy arrived in Nashville from his native Germany. The store has gone well through several generations.

You may remember the fourth generation of Ralph and A. J. Levy, Jr. You may remember seeing their television commercials. They came into the family business after serving in the United States military during World War II. Ralph died in the 1970s, but his son David came into the company. Many generations of Levys have brought real style in men's fashions to Nashville.

Do you remember the Green Hills Market? In 1939, partners A. Roy Greene and Roy T. Primm, Sr. opened their grocery store at 3909 Hillsboro Road. The piece of land they bought for about $5,000 was a cow pasture out in the country.

A couple of years later, Green Hills Market bought the drugstore next door and changed its name to Green Hills

Pharmacy. Soon, a movie theatre was built in the area so it was given the name Green Hills Theatre. I remember, my wife and I saw the movie, *My Fair Lady*, starring Audrey Hepburn and Rex Harrison at the old Green Hills Theatre.

The grocery, the drugstore, and the theatre gave the name Green Hills to that area. And, how that old Nashville meadow has now changed!

After World War II, the growth of Green Hills forced the Green Hills Market to construct a new building. In 1971, they built a new store just behind the old store and it was twice its size.

From "out in the country" to Green Hills, we now enjoy many businesses in that area, and the land is some of the most valuable real estate in our city.

I have happy memories of the old Nashville businesses. Today, we have many helpful high-tech machines to run a business, and we are proud.

But, the old businesses began their operations without computers, fax machines, calculators, cell phones, copy machines, answering machines, and computerized cash registers.

Oh! One more thing. When we called one of those businesses on the telephone, we got to talk to a person instead of listening to a machine give us a menu such as, "Press one if you want billing, press two if you want service, press three if you…" Oh! Shut up!

"It's Fun to Shop at Harvey's"

Writing this column for the *Westview* Newspaper has opened opportunities for me to see old friends, and to make new friends.

I had the opportunity to speak at the Hillwood Country Club for a meeting of the Armed Forces Officers' Wives Club. My wife and I were invited to their meeting where we were served a delicious lunch after which I spoke on "Nashville Nostalgia."

During my talk, I made mention of the great apple pie that we used to eat at Kleeman's restaurant downtown on Sixth Avenue. I made the statement that when Kleeman's closed, Fred Harvey received the recipe for their Harvey's Downstairs Dinette. Then, I simply said, "Since Harvey's is now closed, I wonder where that old recipe is?"

After I had finished speaking to the group, one of the members of the Club came up to me, introduced herself, and said that she was a friend of Fred Harvey, Jr. She looked up his telephone number and said, "Why don't you call him." So, I did.

What a delightful conversation I had with Mr. Fred Harvey, Jr. We talked about a lot of nostalgic things with regard to one of the finest department stores that Nashvillians have ever experienced.

In the early 1940s, Fred Harvey, Sr. brought to Nashville "The store that will never know completion." This department store went into the space which used to be old Lebeck Brothers store on Church Street, and as time went on, Harvey's expanded into the adjoining buildings enlarging Harvey's which eventually covered a full block on Church Street.

Harvey's installed the first escalators in Middle Tennessee. The decorated window displays at Harvey's during Christmas time were the talk of the town. Also, at Christmas time Harvey's sponsored the magnificent display of the glowing, white lighted Nativity Scene located beside the Parthenon in Centennial Park for the enjoyment of the citizens of Nashville and beyond.

All of us remember the trademark of Harvey's as being horses and parts of a carousel. They were painted red, purple, and all wild colors. Then, Mr. Harvey told me something that I didn't know. Those original carousel horses came from the old carousel in Glendale Park which closed in 1932.

The old, dismantled Glendale Park carousel was found in an old barn, and Harvey's bought them. The pieces were painted wild colors and placed in the stores.

What a flood of nostalgic happiness deluged my mind when I realized that the old carousel that my sister and I rode in Glendale Park was the same as we used to see in Harvey's department store!

Fred Harvey, Jr. became an expert on carousel artistry and went around buying many pieces. He placed pieces in all eleven of their stores. Mr. Harvey told me that the finest carousel pieces which he brought to the stores were done by German artisans.

On the third floor of Harvey's downtown store, you may remember another real carousel which the children could ride. Mr. Harvey mentioned that patrons used to give nick-names to the various animals on the ride. For instance, he recalled that the goat was called "Big Red."

Also, on that third floor we enjoyed seeing real live monkeys. In fact, that third floor was called "The Monkey Bar." That is where all of the children's apparel was located.

Mr. Harvey told me that when he sold the stores, he presented one of the old, original Glendale Park carousel horses to Glendale School which is at the location of the old Glendale Park in Nashville.

Mr. Harvey told me that the Kleeman's recipe for apple pie happened like this. Harvey's hired for their Downstairs Dinette the old pastry cook who had worked at Kleeman's. She was an elderly lady who refused to give anyone the recipe.

Harvey's had other younger people working in the kitchen too, and they were not able to find out the recipe either. Harvey's even had the state to analyze the pie. However, Mr. Harvey said that he felt they came pretty close to that old recipe for apple pie.

"Mr. Harvey, I can tell you personally that I have had the apple pie at both Kleeman's and at Harvey's Downstairs Dinette. You succeeded in bringing that good apple pie to Harvey's."

In 1988, Harvey's stores were sold to Peebles. We were no longer able to walk through one of the great department stores in Nashville's history.

Just from that one conversation with Mr. Fred Harvey, Jr., I realized that he is one of the finest exponents of successful department store marketing in the world. Also, he is a gracious and interesting gentleman and a pleasing conversationalist.

And, that is why we always knew that "It's fun to shop at Harvey's."

Walter Sharp's Vision

All of us are proud of the Nashville Symphony Orchestra. I have wonderful memories of the very beginnings of our present orchestra.

The first effort to form a Nashville Symphony Orchestra was in 1904 when J. Hough Guest directed a 38-piece orchestra, playing its first concert on November 18, 1904 at the Vendome Theatre.

Another Nashville Symphony Orchestra was formed in 1920 when an orchestra of 60 pieces was conducted by Professor F. Arthur Henkel who was a music professor at the old Ward-Belmont College.

I have seen pictures of this orchestra at the Nashville Association of Musicians building. I know that Professor Henkel conducted the 60-piece orchestra on the stage of the old Princess Theatre on Church Street.

However, I want to tell about the beginnings of our present orchestra which was formed in 1946 and is still going in a wonderful way.

During the year 1946, I was a music student at George Peabody College which had an outstanding department of music. The prestigious music faculty made the Peabody College music program one of the nation's finest. Much of this can be attributed to the head of the music department at that time, Dr. Irving Wolfe. Also, there were some other fine music programs in surrounding colleges.

The vision of another leader of the arts in Nashville was Mr. Walter Sharp who allowed his vision to include a fine symphony orchestra for Nashville. Mr. Sharp raised a great deal of money, and acquired a charter. Then, the orchestra's first conductor was hired.

In 1946, William Strickland was named conductor. He came with some very admirable credentials. Strickland was organist at New York's Calvary Episcopal Church at age 17. He won a fellowship to Columbia University, and another one to Trinity College of Music in London. Strickland earned a reputation as one of the nation's finest organists before turning to conducting.

We have heard the name William Strickland associated with architecture in Nashville. It was a William Strickland who designed and oversaw the construction of Tennessee's State Capitol building back in the mid 1800s. He is buried in a vault in one of its walls. He also designed the Downtown Presbyterian Church which stands at the corner of Fifth Avenue, North and Church Street.

And, yes, this musical director, William Strickland from Ohio, did claim kinship to the architect which made his closeness to Nashville even more interesting.

Back in 1946, auditions were held to select an orchestra of high quality. Many music faculty members and advanced students from the area were hired to play in the first orchestra under Maestro Strickland.

After a full orchestra was hired, there were regular rehearsals held each week. Sometimes the rehearsals were held in the large studio C of radio station WSM. Sometimes the orchestra rehearsed at the YMHA building which was adjacent and attached to the National Life & Accident Insurance Company building at Seventh and Union where the WSM studios were located.

My clarinet teacher, Professor C. B. Hunt, Jr. was hired as the principal clarinetist. Then, the very next year, Professor Hunt took a leave-of-absence from the symphony and teaching at Peabody to work on his doctor's degree at UCLA in California. I auditioned, and was hired as the symphony's principal clarinetist.

The following year, Professor Hunt informed Peabody and the symphony that he needed to stay at UCLA one more year to continue work on his Ph.D. So, proudly, I got to serve two years as the principal clarinetist with the orchestra.

For the first few years, all of the symphony's subscription concerts were played in the War Memorial Auditorium. Later, some rehearsals and concerts were moved to the Ryman Auditorium. Today, the orchestra performs at TPAC (Tennessee Performing Arts Center) which was built at the site where the old Andrew Jackson Hotel and the Elk's Club stood on Sixth Avenue, North. Soon, the orchestra will move into the new Symphony Hall under construction in lower downtown near the Cumberland River.

The orchestra's quality gained enough recognition in the music world during the late 1940s that *Look* Magazine came to town to take pictures and write a story following the October 1948 concert.

The symphony has had only six principal music directors to this time. They are William Strickland, Guy Taylor, Willis Page, Thor Johnson, Michael Charry, and our present maestro, Kenneth Schermerhorn.

I am grateful to say that I got to play as a clarinetist or bass clarinetist with our symphony off and on for about 25 years. I got to play under three of these conductors, Strickland, Page, and Johnson. My wife, Sonia, sang in the Nashville Symphony Chorus until age 75 which was quite an achievement.

In Nashville, our orchestras, churches, choruses, opera, ballet, drama groups, fine arts, the Parthenon, recording industry, publishing, and our many institutions of higher learning continue to make us proud that, in addition to being Music City USA, we can still declare our great city as "The Athens of the South."

E.D. Thompson, c. 1960s

Just a-Sittin' and a-Rockin'

Sometimes I long for the George Peabody College for Teachers which once was. Right after many of us returned from the service in World War II, the Peabody College campus was flooded with veterans. I think the campus took on a unique air that probably can never be reproduced.

Peabody's music department in which I was enrolled had many veterans as students. Some characteristics of these students that made the department unique were (1) we were older since we had spent some time in the service, (2) we came on campus already as pretty good musicians, (3) we had been through such a life in the service that we were cocky, (4) we had confidence, and (5) we understood the word discipline.

The Peabody music department was very strong because of a very distinguished faculty. I am grateful that I had the opportunity to study with some of the finest music faculty in the country.

The summer sessions at Peabody were the greatest. Our southern climate mixed with the southern laid-back attitudes of the students allowed a relaxed and happy environment for study.

We students would often remark that some of our greatest learning took place in the rocking chairs out on the front porch of the Social-Religious Building. Between classes many students, as well as faculty members, would sit and discuss a great variety of topics.

For instance, a freshman music major could sit and talk with a graduate music student who may have been working on his doctorate. We got book learning and lectures, but we also got practical ideas and hands on usage.

There were many opportunities to hear, as well as participate in, great concerts by the music department faculty and students. All of the summer concerts were held out on the open stage in front of the SR Building overlooking the beautiful campus.

During the summers, we were in the company of many guest artists and teachers. I remember one concert in which I played clarinet in an ensemble. We performed Stravinsky's *L'Histoire du Soldat*. The conductor was the famed musicologist and writer, Nicholas Solimsky.

There were some good players in the ensemble. The oboe player was Nashvillian Elden Gatwood who was playing in the Pittsburgh Symphony. The violinist in the ensemble was Lorin Maazel who later became the conductor of the Pittsburgh Symphony, and today is the conductor of the New York Philharmonic.

Every Sunday evening, the Peabody Vesper services were held on the outdoor stage in front of the Social-Religious Building which today has been renamed the Vanderbilt Wyatt Center. When I sang in the Vesper Choir, our director was Louis Nicholas, an outstanding vocalist and teacher who continued to live in Nashville for many years until recently, when in his 90s, he moved to

Memphis to be closer to his family. In that choir we performed very good literature and were well rehearsed.

Each summer the music department presented an opera. It was well staged with sets and costumes. Excellent vocal music majors sang all of the parts plus there was a fine chorus and orchestra.

Each Fourth of July, the entire college sponsored a big watermelon cutting on campus. The faculty cut and served the melons, and the student body really pigged out on watermelon in an atmosphere of great fun and fellowship. Summers at Peabody were a treat.

Proms were a big thing on campus during the year. I have wonderful memories of one particular prom when Charlie Spivak and His Orchestra played. I had just met my future wife, Sonia Anne Young, in an English class, but we had not started dating.

For this prom, I remember that I escorted the young lady who was the president of the Peabody student body, but I spent most of the evening breaking in and dancing with Sonia. That prom has to remain in my memories.

My wife and I have attended two reunions at Peabody. We enjoyed being back with some great, old friends. And, we did some more a-sittin' and a-rockin' and a-talkin' on the porch of the old Social-Religious Building.

WSM Radio, "We Shield Millions"

WSM's magnificent radio tower, located on Concord Road off of Franklin Pike helped give the radio station its name, "The Air Castle of the South."

Back in the late 1940s, when I had the opportunity to play some at WSM as a musician, the radio station was on the top floor of the National Life & Accident Insurance Company at the corner of Seventh Avenue, North and Union Street.

Radio stations back in the Golden Age of Radio needed a lot of space. Other than the need of three large studios from which to do live broadcasts, a radio station had to have much office space for writers, producers, directors, musicians, commercial sales personnel, office staff, and more. In addition, WSM had a large music library to catalog and store all of the many recordings, musical arrangements used by the live orchestras, and facilities to log all music performed on the air. Mr. Vito Pellettieri was the music librarian at WSM back in the old days.

There were many broadcasts that went out over the NBC radio network from Nashville. The music conductors were Beasley Smith, Pete Brecia, and later, Owen Bradley and Marvin Hughes.

Francis Craig and His Orchestra had an NBC broadcast every Sunday night at 11:05 PM following five minutes of NBC News. You could hear one of the great announcers at WSM such as Jud Collins, Lionel Rico, David Cobb, Ott Devine, Ralph Christian, Ernie Keller, Irving Waugh, and others with pear-shaped tones announce, "Francis Craig's Sunday Night Serenade." Snooky Lanson, Cecil Bailey (a saxophonist in the orchestra,) and Bob Lamm were three of his vocalists, among others.

Each Sunday afternoon a special Lion Oil Network was developed across southern states to broadcast a show called *Sunday Down South.* This show featured a large studio orchestra conducted by Beasley Smith, with singers Snooky Lanson, Dottie Dillard, Anita Kerr, and others.

It is amazing how many great stars at one time or another came through WSM radio.

Dorothy Lamour sang with Francis Craig's Orchestra after singing with Herbie Kaye's band. Dorothy went on to Hollywood and made many of the "road" pictures with Bing Crosby and Bob Hope.

Back in the 1920s, when Francis Craig and His Orchestra played a prom at the University of Georgia in Athens, Georgia, a young fellow came up to Francis and asked if he could join his band. Francis asked him what he played. He told him that he played saxophone. Francis said, "We have enough saxophone players, but I need a singer. Do you sing?" The young fellow said, "Yes, I sing too."

So, after the job that night, Francis had this fellow sing a couple of songs for him. Francis said that after hearing him sing one song, he knew that he had something.

The next day, this fellow by the name of Jimmy joined the band. He came to Nashville, and for the next three years sang with Francis Craig in the Grill Room of the Hermitage Hotel.

At the same time, Jimmy began studying voice with Professor Gaetano S. DeLuca at the old Nashville Conservatory of Music. You may remember that Jimmy (James Melton) went on to sing with the Metropolitan Opera Company in New York City.

Another saxophone player by the name of Kenny Sargent played in Craig's band. Kenny was also a vocalist. Later, he joined Glen Gray and the Casa Loma Orchestra as a star performer.

Dinah Shore was a spot singer at WSM before going on with Eddie Cantor, the movies, and television. Dinah graduated from Hume-Fogg High School, and went to Vanderbilt University. We knew Dinah as Fannie Rose Shore.

There have been many stories as to how Fannie Rose got the name Dinah. It has been said that Eddie Cantor gave her that name when she went on his show, or some radio executive had her take that name, or Dinah just liked that song and name, along with other stories.

I hope the following is the correct story. Her life ambition was to be a singer. She began singing at WSM radio in Nashville. Then, she sold everything she owned to raise funds to go to New York and try to make it big.

She got an audition at WNEW radio in New York City. She sat nervously in a room waiting for her name to be called. Finally, when it was her time to audition, she was told to sing the song "Dinah."

Her audition was such a raving success, she was hired and everybody at the radio station immediately started calling her Dinah. Dinah (Fannie Rose) never forgot her roots. She came back to Nashville many times to see her many friends.

People's best memory of her may be when at the end of her TV shows she sang "See the USA in Your Chevrolet," and threw a big kiss to the audience.

Snooky Lanson went on to sing with Ray Noble's Orchestra on the *Charlie McCarthy Show*, and to star on *Your Hit Parade*.

Vocalist Kitty Kallen sang at WSM. I understand, Kitty married Clint Garvin who was a saxophone player in the Francis Craig Orchestra. Kitty later had such hit recordings as "I'm Beginning to See the Light" and "It's Been a Long, Long Time" with Harry James and His Orchestra.

As far as other band singers at WSM, there were two brothers with the last name of Johnston. Both of them changed their names. Bob changed his name only slightly to Bob Johnstone, and went on to sing with several name bands, one of which was Shep Fields and His Orchestra. His brother, Howard, changed his name to Gene Howard, and went on to sing with the Teddy Powell, Bob Chester, and Stan Kenton orchestras.

Anita Kerr became quite famous through her recordings with the "Anita Kerr Singers."

There were a number of early recordings made in old Studio C at WSM, and not just country songs. Songwriter and band leader Francis Craig recorded "Red Rose" and "Beg Your Pardon," among others.

He hit big in 1947 with his song and recording of "Near You." A real plus was when Mr. Television, Milton Berle, began to use "Near You" as his theme song.

Marjorie Cooney was one of the women pioneers in radio when she played such a big role at WSM radio.

Marge was at WSM with such old-timers as station manager Harry Stone. One of her first roles on the air was with Beasley Smith when they played a program called *The Piano Twins*. Jack Harris was the news director when Marge auditioned and was selected for a news program to be sponsored by the Faultless Starch Company. She became the host of *A Woman Looks at the News*. Using the air name Ann Ford, Marge also was the host of an interview program at WSM called *The Man I Married*. Marge was a great lady. She passed away on Saturday, February 17, 2001, at age 95.

My friend and a mainstay at WSM is retired Elmer Alley who was quite an influence in the development of WSM. One day we enjoyed reminiscing about some of the old singing groups at WSM. For instance, do you remember the "Vagabonds?" Their big song was "Lamp Lighting Time in the Valley."

Also, there was a singing group called "Jack, Nap and Dee." They sang on a lot of live programs. Jack in the group was Jack Shook who played guitar in the staff orchestra. Jack played a left-handed acoustic guitar back before electric guitars seemed to take over. Jack recorded with Bing Crosby and many others.

Do you remember "Betty and the Dixie Dons" who sang on WSM radio? You might remember Dr. Humphrey Bate's Possum Hunters who played on the *Grand Ole Opry*. Dr. Bate's daughter was Alcyon Bate Beasley. When Alcyon sang with Jack, Nap and Dee, they were known as "Betty and the Dixie Dons."

In our reminiscing, it would be impossible to mention all of the country stars who went through WSM and the *Grand Ole Opry*. The Opry was and is one of the greatest examples of radio success in the history of radio!

For many years on the station-break at the insurance company's WSM radio station, when the announcer would give the call letters, you would hear him say, "We shield millions."

WSM came on the air in 1925, and that phrase above was used from the beginning. For the inaugural program, Mr. C. A. Craig, the insurance company's president, dedicated the station to public service, while Tennessee Governor Austin Peay offered his congratulations on this new undertaking.

Edwin W. Craig, who was the vice-president of National Life, reportedly said, "This is station WSM... We shield millions... Owned and operated by the National Life & Accident Insurance Company, Nashville, Tennessee."

That first program on WSM included musical performances by Francis Craig's Columbia Recording Orchestra, and Beasley Smith's Andrew Jackson Hotel Orchestra. Others performing on that historic day were baritone Joseph MacPherson, the Fisk Jubilee Singers, the Al Menah's Shrine Band, and the Knights of Columbus Vocal Quartet.

In October of 2000, WSM radio celebrated its big 75th anniversary. From the beginnings, WSM radio was synonymous with the word QUALITY.

Today, WSM radio (650 AM) is primarily a country music station. But, when I played my horn in old Studio C back in the late forties, I think of WSM as classical music, big bands, superstars, the *Grand Ole Opry*, "We shield millions," and the "Air Castle of the South."

The Blizzard of '51

Often I will hear someone refer to a horrible winter when ice covered the ground, tree branches were iced over, and power lines were down. Someone will top that by remembering that terrible storm back in the 80s. Another will be reminded of that real bad winter in the 70s. Many of us had problems in one of the bad winters of the 90s.

But, after all is said and done, everything these people had mentioned was just a mild skirmish.

Many of you Nashvillians, along with I, will remember what we believe to be the storm of the century. The winter of January and February of 1951 is what we still refer to as "The Blizzard of '51." I remember it well.

It all began on the afternoon of Sunday, January 28, 1951. When it started, we Nashvillians, familiar with the two-inch snows which are here today and gone tomorrow, thought nothing about it. Many times we Nashvillians saw snow in the morning which closed the schools, the snow would turn to slush in the afternoon, and schools would reopen the next morning.

But, the Blizzard of '51, not so!

The snow of Sunday, January 28th was beautiful. Not too much traffic to worry about. No schools anyway. But, the snow didn't melt!

Monday, January 29, 1951, no schools! I was teaching at Hillsboro High School at the time. Monday was dark and cold. The snow was not melting.

On Tuesday, January 30, there was another inch or so of snow, and this time there was also a glaze of sleet.

The Blizzard of '51 hit like a snow shovel in our faces on Wednesday night, January 31. *The Tennessean* reported, "It was something that Nashville had never seen in recorded times. A massive ice storm."

Howling winds accompanied by freezing rain covered the city. Tree branches were sagging under ice. Electric wires and telephone lines looked like long, sagging ribbons of ice. It didn't take long for the lines to snap. No telephones! No electric power in many places!

On Thursday morning, February 1, the storm had let up, but the temperature in Nashville had dropped to one below zero. Nashville was shut down.

The airport was closed. More than a third of the city was without electricity. Water pipes were freezing and bursting.

In 1951, passenger trains were still serving Nashville, but an agent at Union Station said that most trains were about 18 hours late, and he really didn't know where many of them were, because the telegraph and telephone lines were down.

By this time, the several layers of snow, sleet, and frozen rain stood at about eight inches and was as hard as concrete.

On Friday morning, February 2, the temperature dropped to 13 degrees below zero.

I can relate a couple of personal stories during this time. I was dating Sonia, who later would become my wife. We had tickets to a concert by Fred Waring and the Pennsylvanians at the War Memorial Auditorium.

Before the streets completely closed down, I decided that I would take a city bus to Sonia's house. I couldn't even think about getting my car out of the driveway. So, I walked to the bus line, took a bus, and walked up to Sonia's house. By this time, we felt that it would be ridiculous to try and get to town and back for the concert. Reluctantly, we were not able to use our tickets to the concert.

Sonia and I just stayed at her house as we watched the snow and ice get worse and worse.

Finally, I figured that I had better try to get a bus back home. The cold and ice were getting worse.

Somehow my bus driver was able to move that bus over the ice. It was some slippery ride. When the bus got to downtown, who should get on the bus but my old music professor from Peabody College, Professor Louis Nicholas. He had gone to the Fred Waring concert. At that time, Mr. Nicholas was the music critic for *The Tennessean*. He told me that the concert was wonderful, but there was only a handful of people in the audience.

Thankfully, that experienced city bus driver got Mr. Nicholas safely to his stop, and then on to mine. I was home at last.

I was teaching at Hillsboro High School, and it was between the first and second semesters. In addition to teaching band at Hillsboro, I was teaching a sophomore English class for that year.

I was talking on the telephone to the Hillsboro principal, Mr. John Koen. He said that he wished he had all of the grades in so he could be handling that part of his semester's work. I thought he wanted my grades. I offered to get out and walk them over to him. But, then he said, "Oh no! Yours alone wouldn't help. I need the grades from all teachers and all classes."

Well, we lived through it. I kept my feet up toward the grate at my house in which I burned coal. I didn't get COLD!

So, when someone begins to tell you about that horrible winter and storm of the 70s, 80s, and 90s, just smile, and say, "I was in the Mother of all Nashville storms. I was in the Blizzard of '51!"

How Did Tex Ritter Get in This?

It was back when Nashville was growing as a music industry town. Anyone who had a song that had promise at all was an instant music publisher. All a songwriter had to do was get a song recorded by a big artist, and that songwriter was able to pay the bills off pretty quickly.

Of course, "All one had to do" is not a good choice of words, because it was a pretty tall order to get a song recorded by a big artist. Thousands of songwriters came to Nashville with a guitar and that "great song." After a few years, most of them had to head back home to the farm, office, school, or wherever. Breaking into the music business was not easily done. Most all of those promising songwriters and singers often were told, "Don't give up your day job!"

Back in those days, my wife and I had returned to Nashville after spending some time in teaching. I won't go into how teachers were so poorly paid back then, because we shall never regret the years that we spent in teaching young people.

Upon our return to Nashville, we were making it very well but with very little money. I opened Thompson Music House as a music service company. I wrote lead sheets for songwriters, our whole family went into studios and made demo recordings for clients, I did copy work, made sheet music arrangements, arranged for choral and instrumental groups, and did some composing.

Thompson Music House did some publishing, too. My hymn titled, "Thy Peace for Us," is published in five different church hymnals.

So, I set up business at Tex Ritter's restaurant on West End Avenue at the corner of Twenty-first Avenue near Vanderbilt University. It was a great layout for a restaurant and a music office!!

Later, the old Tex Ritter's restaurant was torn down, and a new Pizza Hut was built at that spot. Today, the Qdoba Restaurant stands at 21st and West End.

Every morning back in those days, I went into Tex Ritter's place and got a cup of coffee. The back table was somewhat isolated and removed from other people. Right there by the table was a pay telephone where I could call out. Also, I could give the phone number to those who needed to call me.

When I completed a job, the restaurant was where I met my clients. It was right in the center of town which was an excellent location for most people. So, a table, a chair, a pay telephone, and a briefcase was all I needed to operate the music business. Of course, I would go home each day, take some manuscript paper, and begin to write whatever the job called for.

People often asked me, "Was Tex Ritter ever there in the restaurant?" I answered, "Oh, he certainly was." And, I must say that I stood in awe being in his presence.

As a kid, I saw the great Tex Ritter in western movies. You might remember that Tex sang the theme song in the 1952 movie, *High Noon*, which starred Gary Cooper and

Grace Kelly. The song was "Do Not Forsake Me, Oh, My Darling" written by Dmitri Tiomkin.

Yes, Tex was a very big movie star. Sometimes I would sit there in the restaurant at my table, look up and see Tex, and find it hard to believe that I was right there looking at Tex Ritter.

Some people would say, "I didn't know if he came in there, or they just used his name for the restaurant."

Oh, no! Tex was there. He was getting rather old, and he was pretty much retired, but he loved to be around people.

Many times I saw Tex talk to families that came into the restaurant, and he would ask them if they wanted to go to the *Grand Ole Opry*. They would say "yes," and then Tex would go to the pay phone (my office pay phone by the back table), and call the Opry to get tickets reserved for them.

What a thrill that must have been for people to go back home and mention to their friends that Tex Ritter got their Opry tickets for them.

Tex Ritter loved people. He loved to talk. He was getting older, but he still appeared on the Opry and other engagements at times.

But, do you know that a lot of the younger people really didn't know the thrill it should have been to be in the presence of such a great star? I saw some young people be so disrespectful to Tex. It broke my heart.

Those young people just saw Tex as an old man. But, I sat there and saw an image of a great cowboy sitting on his horse which filled the large silver screen every Saturday at the matinee that my sister and I used to attend.

Tex was always glad to help out at any occasion when he was needed. Once, he even sang on a concert with the

Nashville Youth Orchestra. Andrew Ponder, a professor in the music department at George Peabody College, was the conductor of the orchestra at that time. Professor Ponder told me that the concert with Tex Ritter was the most popular and successful of all the orchestra's events.

Once I needed to go to Tex Ritter's home. I went over to deliver a cancer insurance policy.

During the time that I was playing in bands, playing in the symphony, directing a church choir, and trying to build my music business, I sold cancer insurance policies to help augment our family income. I got a letter out to all members of local 257 of the Nashville Association of Musicians, and a lot of them wanted to buy the cancer policy.

I wrote the policy for a number of musicians. I even sold some of the artists such as Tex Ritter. Barbara Mandrell's family bought one. I sold one to Sonny James, and I remember that I delivered one to Don Gibson and his wife at their condo in Bellevue. Don Gibson is that great songwriter who wrote "O Lonesome Me" and "I Can't Stop Loving You," among others.

I also delivered one of the cancer policies to Roy Acuff, Jr. and to "Lightning" Chance who was Roy Acuff's bass man in his Smokey Mountain Boys.

I remember that I got a policy for Jimmy Riddle. Jimmy was the fine harmonica player on the Opry. Oh, there were artists Vic Willis, Carl Smith, and a lot of musicians.

I remember the day that I delivered the policy to Tex. The Ritters lived in a beautiful home over on Franklin Pike. It was Tex, his wife, and their son Tom who lived there. Their other son, John Ritter, was already out in Hollywood.

I nervously walked up to the front door and knocked. Tex's son, Tom, first monitored the caller. When Tex heard what it was about, he came to the door and asked me in. I walked into their attractively decorated living room which was very rustic, much like an old ranch house.

I recall that I was very nervous as I sat there trying to talk. Like I said, I was in awe at being in the presence of this great movie star. But, Tex was totally laid back carrying on a conversation with me.

I handed Tex the cancer policy and was ready to go. But, it seemed like Tex wanted to sit and talk on and on. That's why I know that he liked to talk to people.

When Tex died, we lost a legend and a great American gentleman.

When Tex died, I reported the news to my wife. For just a few moments, silence dwelt in our room as we reflected with compassion, I guess upon all people and, in fact, the whole world. Tex was gone.

There Are All Different Kinds of Victories!

As a Boy Scout back in the late 1930s and the early 1940s, along with my friends, I participated in many enjoyable experiences. Some of those happy moments were getting to usher at the Vanderbilt football games at Dudley Field.

Scouts from all over Middle Tennessee would assemble at the stadium early on Saturday mornings to get instructions on ushering people to their seats for the game.

During the morning of a home game, there would be an inspection of all Scouts. Our Scout leaders made certain that our uniforms were being worn properly, our haircuts were up to standard, and everything about us was up to the standard of presenting ourselves well before the public.

We were taught the location of every seat in all of the sections in the stadium. We were able to seat people immediately, accurately, professionally, and with a polite, cheerful, and courteous attitude.

All during the week, we had a love for playing football of the sandlot style. But, on Saturdays, we got to see Vandy play such teams as L. S. U., Tennessee, Ole Miss, and others.

Back in those days, the first Vanderbilt home game each season was against Sewanee. The real name of the school is The University of the South, but it goes by the name Sewanee. Vanderbilt usually won the victory over Sewanee.

The old Dudley Stadium is still there even though some nice modifications and enhancements have been added.

The first two times Billy Graham brought his Crusade to Nashville, it was held at Dudley Field. The first Crusade was in August of 1954. I am sorry that I was unable to attend that first one. My wife and I had just married, and we were teaching in South Carolina. My mother and sister attended the Crusade, and they wrote us a long letter as to how wonderful it was for them to be present at the Crusade.

One thing I do remember about the 1954 Crusade was that old Dudley Stadium for the first time was lit up with high powered lights. This was something I never saw as a Boy Scout ushering at the games which were always played on Saturday afternoons.

Back in 1954, the Billy Graham Crusade donated a payment to the university for the permanent lights on the field in exchange for free rent at Dudley Stadium.

My wife, my son, my daughter, and I did attend the second Billy Graham Crusade at Dudley Field in 1979. As I sat in that old stadium some forty years after ushering at the Vandy games as a Boy Scout, my mind reflected on the old times. I got to see some great football games and some great victories on that field by some outstanding Vanderbilt players and coaches. Before each game, the public address system was roaring with Francis Craig's "Dynamite," Vandy's fight song, which is still used today.

Since that first and second Billy Graham Crusade, the Crusade has made giant steps.

My wife, my son, and I went to the last Billy Graham Crusade held in the Coliseum in June of 2000. If Crusades of the past were inspirational, you can imagine the manifestations of this last one.

We enjoyed hearing The Bill Gaither Vocal Band plus his television *Homecoming Friends.* We once again got to hear George Beverly Shea sing. This time he was more than 90 years old.

After the many years, Cliff Barrows was still directing the Crusade Choir. At the Crusade we attended in 1979, the choir was made up of approximately 2,000 singers. On this Crusade of the year 2000, Cliff directed a choir of 5,000 singers.

After other musical witnessing, and short comments from our governor, Don Sundquist, and Nashville mayor, Bill Purcell, The Reverend Billy Graham was introduced. The highlight of the evening was seeing and hearing this American Icon who is one of the legendary religious figures of the last and this century.

We saw our Tennessee Titans execute the Music City Miracle in the game against the Buffalo Bills on this same ball field, and go on to the Super Bowl. On this Titans football field during the Billy Graham Crusade, I am sure there were even more miracles which occurred in people's lives that can go on to even greater victories. There are all different kinds of victories.

Role Models Make a Difference

The Athens of the South is a city in which we can be very proud. This heraldic insignia was not bestowed upon Nashville only because a replica of the Parthenon was built to celebrate our centennial year of 1896.

We also were honored with this label because of some other wonderful Neo-Grecian architectural structures, our churches, the culture the city has always attempted to foster, and because of the many colleges and universities which have played a great role in the development, culture, and progress of our city.

When I was growing up, Tennessee State University was called Tennessee A&I which stood for Agricultural and Industrial colleges. The university had great strength and grew.

I have been interested in TSU because my son teaches on the faculty there. I have seen my son as a teacher work in the lives of the students. For instance, one of his students said, "If it had not been for Mr. Thompson working with me and encouraging me, I would have dropped out of school all together." That is a strong testimonial. And, there are many other examples.

There are and have been many role models at Tennessee State University who have made a difference. I had the pleasure of knowing or working with some fine musicians from TSU in years gone by.

I remember the late Dr. W. O. Smith with whom I played in the Nashville Symphony. W. O. played viola in the orchestra. Prior to that time in Nashville, W. O. also played string bass and had such credentials as having performed with Bessie Smith, Dizzy Gillespie, and Lucky Millinder. W. O. played on Coleman Hawkins' classic 1939 Bluebird recording of "Body and Soul."

Dr. Smith was the founder of the W. O. Smith Nashville Community School of Music for underprivileged children which is still in progress.

I worked with pianist Leonard Morton who later became the music supervisor for the Metropolitan Schools.

I was in the band teaching profession when Don Q. Pullen of TSU had an outstanding band program at the old Washington Junior High School. Don had many proteges such as drummer Morris Palmer, bass player Charles Dungey, and Kay Roberts. Kay was a violinist in the Nashville Symphony, then studied conducting in college, and later came back to Nashville and guest conducted the Nashville Symphony.

Also, Marcus Gunter was the band director at old Pearl High School at the same time I was the band director at Hillsboro High School.

I remember Louis Smith, a music teacher at TSU who was a fine trumpet player and arranger. Andy Goodrich was an outstanding saxophone player at the school.

Back in the early 1950s, I recall a weekend of dances at TSU. At that time, I was playing with Tommy Knowles and His Orchestra. We played a dance in the cafeteria area one night. Following our dance, we went over to the gymnasium where another dance was being played by Lionel Hampton and His Orchestra.

There was a fine trombone player in the university band from Wartrace, Tennessee by the name of Jimmy Cleveland. Later, when Lionel Hampton heard Jimmy play, he wanted him to join his band.

So, in 1950, Jimmy went with Lionel Hampton's band for about three years. Jimmy Cleveland also played with Johnny Richards' band at Birdland in New York City, Jimmy made some records with Dizzy Gillespie, and in 1959-60, Jimmy toured Europe with Quincy Jones. Jimmy was in the presence of some pretty strong musicians!

Tennessee State's Ed Temple coached Wilma Rudolph, and the famous Tigerbelles to achieve many awards in the Olympics. Another TSU athlete, broad-jump star Ralph Boston, also was an Olympic Gold Medal winner in 1960.

Let me mention one more person from TSU who contributed much to the lives of students over the years. One day I was in the Waffle House out on Charlotte Pike when John Merritt came in. He said that he was on the way to Dickson to help recruit a football player for Tennessee State University.

John's presence in the building with his smile, cheerful talk, and his personality converted the entire restaurant to an upbeat and happy environment. We know how he contributed to the lives of his football players and students under him when he coached T S U football.

It dawned on me. Every state, city, and community in our country has problems that people want to fix. And, all we really need is a lot more role models.

Big Bands, Beautiful Ballads, and Great Groups

One afternoon in 1971, I was slowly turning my radio dial over the AM band, and all of a sudden I heard a tape of the old *Fibber McGee and Molly* radio show. Being an old radio buff, I had to listen to it. Following that show, the station began to play big band music. I was hooked!

I soon learned that the radio station was WAMB, and the station was dedicated to playing old-time radio programs and music of the big bands. The Golden Era of the Big Bands lasted roughly from the 1930s until the early 1950s. This was the great music of the World War II Era.

Radio station WAMB came on the air in April of 1971. The owner is Mr. Bill Barry. The station came on the air with only 250 watts daytime. With Bill Barry's expertise, the station advanced to 5,000 watts, then to 25,000, and finally to 50,000 watts as it is today, and now broadcasting 24 hours a day in stereo. The station can be heard at 1160 on the AM dial, and 98.7 on the FM dial.

There could not be a better person than Bill Barry to operate such a nostalgic radio station as WAMB, the big band station.

Bill Barry's life was immersed with big bands, good music, and radio. In fact, much of Bill's life parallels my own. Bill had his own high school dance orchestra before World War II when he was a student at Castle Heights Military Academy in Lebanon, Tennessee.

Bill had a college dance orchestra when he was at Vanderbilt University. In a conversation with Bill, he told me that he remembers the last job the band played. It was for a Vanderbilt fraternity dance at the old Maxwell House Hotel in 1950.

Bill Barry is qualified to be in radio as he possesses a vast amount of experience. Back in 1957 with friend, Bill Baird, they owned station WFMB. At that time, it was the only FM station in town. They sold the station in 1964. Today, that station is WLAC-FM.

Also, Bill Barry worked with other properties. You may remember station WWGM (Wonderful World of Good Music.) Later, that station became a gospel music station with studios over on Blair Boulevard.

In 1976, Bill entered another good music station which you may remember. It was WZEZ-FM. Bill also took old WENO radio in 1995 and put it back on the air.

You probably remember a good station in town with the call letters WMAK. Bill put that station back on the air, and leased it to TV channel 5 which also operated channel 50. At that time, we could hear the TV broadcast over this radio station WMAK, 1430 on the AM dial. Later, the station served the community as a Spanish speaking station.

WAMB has had some great announcers over the years including the present ones. Going back over the years, you heard a fellow I can remember only as Moby. Other announcers were Joe Martin, Bart Walker, Elizabeth Comfort, and Bill Jones.

You heard the great radio voice and humor of Joe Holcomb who has passed away. Also, you may remember Buzz Benson, also deceased. I first knew of Buzz when he was at station WSIX and had a record show called *Dusty Discs*.

You should remember another announcer, Bob Sticht, who had a wonderful weekly program on WAMB with Snooky Lanson of Francis Craig's Orchestra and *Your Hit Parade* fame.

Another great voice at WAMB was that of Ken Bramming. Ken also has passed away. You may remember him when he was playing great music at WSM-FM. Ken was also the program director at WAMB before his passing.

The present roster of great announcers includes one who has been with WAMB almost from the start. I shall have to single out Brother Howard Wilks. He does the gospel show every Sunday morning, and has a wonderful following.

Other present announcers on the WAMB roster are Jack Gallo, Bill Brittain, Mike Robbins, Ron Johnson, Bill Barry, Bill Baird, Dick Cowl, and Jeff Thompson.

I have to be a little partial to the last name since he is my son. Jeff is on the faculty at Tennessee State University teaching English and Writing Skills. He also works part-time on radio station WAMB. He has played great music there since the 1980s.

Jeff has great shows on Saturday nights from 6 until 10, and Sunday nights from 7 until 10. He does special shows such as remembering and honoring birthdays of great singers and instrumentalists.

Each year during the Academy Awards, Jeff plays the entire list of Academy Award winning songs from the first year to the present. One interesting show was when Jeff went year by year and played the great songs which happened to lose the Academy Award during those years. That show involved some great songs.

Great radio styling and good music have permeated the air waves over the years by way of radio station WAMB. The entire city gives a big thanks to the station which has held on to old-time radio, and the big bands-- radio of yesteryears.

WAMB has served more and more listeners year by year. Today, the station serves the world. All over the world, WAMB can be heard on the Internet at www.broadcastamerica.com and then, just click on "adult standards" to hear big bands, beautiful ballads, and great groups in the world of great music.

Jeff Thompson on WAMB radio, 2003

Montgomery Bell in Nashville's Past

Recently, my family drove down to the newly built Montgomery Bell State Park Inn for a delicious buffet dinner.

Our family had gone to the old Inn many times. You probably went there too for delicious meals, or meetings in the spacious convention room. Twice, I even played dance jobs for the Waverly Cotillion Club in that room.

One year we attended a musical drama in that old room. It was an original drama sponsored by the Christ Presbyterian Church, and performed by excellent Nashville singers and actors.

The old Inn had a steep staircase down from the lobby to the dining room. It was a beautiful sight looking out over the lake and the woods through the Inn's large picture windows. In the winter, it was nice to sit beside the roaring wood fire in the lobby.

Finally, the old Inn was torn down. A new Montgomery Bell Inn sits at that location now. It has many improvements. There is a beautiful dining room, additional space for meetings, and many attractive rooms for staying over-night.

After a delicious buffet dinner at the new Montgomery Bell Park Inn on that day, my family headed back home when my sister suggested that we drive down to The Narrows on the Harpeth River, a site which holds many memories of our past. We turned onto Cedar Hill Road off of U. S. Highway 70 beside the Harpeth River bridge and headed for The Narrows. Even these roads have been changed over the years.

Of course, this was the location of the old Boy Scout Camp Boxwell. I spent camping time there as a Boy Scout. My sister, Elva, first met her husband there while visiting the camp. On this day as we saw the sights, my sister reminisced about the old swinging bridge which stretched across the scenic Harpeth River.

Somehow during that visit many years ago, she walked across the river on that swinging bridge, but she refused to go back across the bridge. That is when her future husband agreed to get a canoe and take her back across the river by boat.

I reminisced about the time I was initiated into the Order of the Arrow at scout camp. As part of our initiation, we had to spend one night outside on the hill above The Narrows tunnel. At other times, we had hikes, great wiener roasts, and outings up on that bluff.

On this recent Sunday outing with my family many years after I had attended Boy Scout Camp Boxwell there, my son and I walked down to The Narrows tunnel which is a very historic site.

Montgomery Bell came to Middle Tennessee in 1802 and went to work for James Robertson at the Cumberland Iron Works. Two years later, he bought Robertson out and proceeded to build Iron Forges all over Middle Tennessee.

Wanting to develop a water-powered mill on the Harpeth River, Bell cut a tunnel through the limestone bluff to divert a surge of water through the hill to power his mill.

Literature tells us that The Narrows tunnel was constructed around 1819. The tunnel is approximately 8 feet high, 16 feet wide, and 209 feet long. The tunnel cuts off a five-mile bend in the river.

The day my son and I looked into the tunnel was following many days of rain. The river was up, and the water going through the tunnel was quite swift.

In 1855, the Western Military Institute was attached to the University of Nashville with the object of establishing a preparatory department for the university. A large and flourishing school soon developed. It almost closed in 1862 when the university buildings were occupied as a military hospital.

In 1867, the trustees of the University of Nashville set about reorganizing this preparatory school. Under terms of a will dated in 1852, the trustees had received a bequest from Mr. Montgomery Bell which was used to establish a permanent endowment for the school.

This preparatory school was reorganized in keeping with the terms of Mr. Bell's will. Montgomery Bell Academy enrolled students in September of 1867.

Until 1881, the school was conducted in the buildings of the university near Rutledge Hill. During that year, the school transferred to quarters bounded by Lindsley Avenue, University Street, and Academy Place, where an excellent brick building was erected.

During the year 1911, the trustees of the university decided to discontinue their medical school, and devote all of the income from their endowment, as well as from their entire remaining property, to the further endowment of Montgomery Bell Academy.

In 1913, the trustees sold the building and grounds of the Academy situated in South Nashville to the City Park Commission. Then, the Academy secured temporary quarters in a building on Seventh Avenue, North.

In the spring of 1914, a 32-acre tract of land on Harding Road was purchased which is the present site of Montgomery Bell Academy.

Mr. Montgomery Bell has been an important entity in the history and growth of Nashville. The Narrows is now under the control of our Park Commission, and Montgomery Bell Academy, named after Bell, has upheld his original purpose of developing a school second to none of its class in the South.

From Meat and Potatoes to Trendy Shopping!

Today, we can drive through Hillsboro Village on 21st Avenue, South and see a totally different Village from what we had back in "the old days."

The Belmont Methodist Church has remained at the corner of Acklen and 21st Avenues. I was a member there before and after my service in the Army during World War II. I moved my membership when I became a choir director at another church.

At the corner of Blakemore and 21st Avenues, on the other end of the business village, we used to see great movies at the Belmont Theatre. The theatre entrance was right at the corner of Blakemore and 21st Avenues. Today, the Educators' Credit Union occupies that restructured building.

In the middle of the block, a few doors up from 21st Avenue on Belcourt Avenue, we enjoyed stage productions at the Nashville Community Playhouse. Back then, the new addition to the building had not been added which made two theatres for the Belcourt Cinema which are there today.

The Nashville Community Playhouse was known for its excellence. How could it not have been with such creative students from Peabody and Vanderbilt which included Delbert Mann and Fred Coe. Later, both of these gentlemen became pioneers in dramatic productions in early television.

Delbert Mann earned a reputation in the early 1950s as one of the premier directors of TV drama. You may remember him doing Paddy Chayefsky's teleplay of *Marty*.

Fred Coe later was the producer for the movie made for television, *The Miracle Worker*, starring Patty Duke.

That theatre location on Belcourt has a lot of nostalgic memories. The Hillsboro Theatre which showed silent movies sat at that location beginning in 1925. Its entrance was on 21st Avenue. In 1931, it became the Children's Theatre of Nashville. The *Grand Ole Opry* played at that location from 1934 until 1936. The theatre took on the name Nashville Community Playhouse after 1937. Then, in 1966 it became the Belcourt Cinema.

Other shops and stores which filled the Village when I was younger were Woolworth (which location is now Bosco's), McClure's (which location is now an antique shop,) a photographic studio, dress shops, and other stores. I remember that the last phonograph needle I ever bought was from a shop in Hillsboro Village.

At the corner of 21st Avenue and Belcourt in the old days was Anthony's Gulf Filling Station. It was operated by Robert Sweeney and Haywood Gwinner. My sister used to date Robert. They both were graduates of Hume-Fogg High School. The old filling station location is now Jackson's Bistro.

At the foot of Acklen Avenue was the Warner Drugstore. It was still there in the late 60s and early 70s when I was teaching at Belmont College. Many days I used to go down there for my lunch which usually consisted of a ham salad sandwich and a chocolate soda. The location of the old Warner Drugstore is now a store called Arts, Antiques and Artifacts.

My musician friend, Dick Cotten, put up his Cotten Music Center in the Village in 1961, and it remains today. After Dick's death, I guess the new owner wanted to keep the same name for the music store.

My wife and I used to eat at the old Pancake Pantry where we were treated to various fruit filled pancakes. The remodeled Pancake Pantry is a thriving business there today catering to many in the music industry.

You probably remember Jones Pet Shop. The old Pet Shop sign still stands above the entrance. However, today that location is Fido's restaurant.

The old Hillsboro Village was a traditional shopping area for neighbors. You could buy gas at Gulf and groceries at H. G. Hill. You could shop in a five-and-ten-cent store. You could eat and see a movie. You could get your prescriptions filled at a drugstore. You could buy clothes and have your picture made.

Today, the area is more faddish and trendy. You can enjoy art shops, antique shops, and bookstores, complimented by specialty shops.

I am not complaining, I'm just saying that it is different. Hillsboro Village is not like it used to be.

When Bellevue Was "Out in the Country"

Some of you old-timers may remember facts about the original Belle Vue log home which was built by the DeMoss family. It stood on a hill overlooking Morton Mill Road which included a beautiful view of the scenic Harpeth River.

Dolly Carter and her family, who owned the log cabin, donated this old Belle Vue Number One to the Bellevue Harpeth Historic Association. Funds were raised to pay for the dismantling and restoration of the cabin.

I was born within the old city limits of Nashville, but the great beauty of the community called Bellevue was present in our lives as we would see and enjoy it when we drove "out in the country."

After I graduated from the music department at Peabody College, I served as the band director at Hillsboro High School on Hillsboro Road in Green Hills from 1948 until 1954.

As the band director, I remember the first time I took the Hillsboro Band to Bellevue High School for the football game between Hillsboro and Bellevue. Back in those days, Bellevue was still a quaint, little town out in the country.

For that football game, the Hillsboro Band loaded the bus and headed out to Bellevue in plenty of time for the game. Apparently, the bus driver didn't know where the Bellevue High School football field was located. When I realized that the bus had passed over bridges on the Harpeth River several times, I saw that I needed to help.

I rushed up to the driver, and told him to turn around. I realized that we could get to Bellevue without going through Centerville, Dickson, and Waverly!!

With just a limited amount of knowledge about the country side, I was able to direct the driver to the Bellevue football field just in time for the kick-off.

I even remember the half-time show that the Hillsboro Band performed at that game. We did a take-off on the old *Dragnet* show with music and lively action of the detectives. I think the people liked it.

A short while back, I had a nice conversation with Bellevue's Betty Hunt. Betty used to play on the old Bellevue High School girl's basketball team. She was telling me about her days on the team when they played half-court.

Back then, girl's basketball had not reached the heights of recognition that it enjoys today. Today, we can see high school games on television. We can see Vanderbilt and Tennessee lady's basketball games played full-court on national television.

Betty was excited talking to me about the 1962 year when Bellevue's girl's basketball team went undefeated for the whole year, and went on to win the district tournament.

In our conversation, Betty mentioned something which proves just how small this world really is. She said, "I remember having to play against Sharon Buchi from Hillsboro High School."

I told Betty that it just so happens that Sharon is my wife's cousin.

The old Bellevue High School was situated up above the football field where the Community Center now sits. When the high school was torn down, they held on to the gymnasium. And, the football field still stands. Yes, the same field that I had to tell the bus driver how to get to in the darkness, out in the country, back around 1950.

My wife and I were born in Nashville. We remember Bellevue as being out in the country as well as now being a tastefully growing community. We are proud to be homeowners and citizens of Bellevue, Tennessee.

We still have some of that old country in the Bellevue area today. Sometimes go down to Newsom Mill. Enjoy the scenery. Listen to the gentle wind blowing over the land. See the trees swaying in the breeze.

Then, go into the quietness of the woods anywhere in Bellevue and see the wild flowers and listen to the birds sing. Then, go stand by the Harpeth River and hear the ripple of the water as it rushes down-stream.

Then, go up Morton Mill Road and enjoy the Bellevue Greenway as you stand and look down through the trees to the scenic Harpeth River below.

But, best of all, it's the people. The southern hospitality flows with each greeting and each compassionate lift when we are in need of some help.

Then, try to tell me that you had rather retire some other place.

Nashville's Glory Lives On

Nashville didn't disappear down some endless corridor of the past,
so we can relive that radiant past while anticipating an exciting future.

Replica of James Robertson's log cabin located in H.G. Hill Park off of Charlotte Pike

West Nashville's Pride Lives On

After the Civil War, the South needed to recover financially. After a number of years, people felt that new industry is what was needed to produce profits. Citizens felt that a new, southern, industrial city could create jobs and money for development and expansion.

The site of the new manufacturing city of the South was chosen. It was decided to develop an industrial town about three miles from the Tennessee state capitol building in Nashville. The new town was to be West Nashville. However, the citizens began to call it simply NEW TOWN.

New Town was to become a center of the charcoal iron business where advantage could be taken of its mineral resources of iron, coal, and hardwood. Also, the town would be located near the cultural center of Nashville.

As time passed, New Town (West Nashville) developed into a number of neighborhoods. Richland Park Neighborhood was one of them.

On the south side of the park, a row of Victorian brick homes were built along Park Avenue. On the north side was the business district.

My mother, father, and other members of their families lived in West Nashville at one time. My grandparents on my father's side lived with pride in Nashville's old West Nashville. In later times, I visited my grandmother and other relatives a great deal, so that is why I have a definite love for West Nashville.

My dear grandmother was a strong, religious lady who helped shape the lives of many people. She lived across the street from her beloved church in which she played a major role.

In the old days, her family's church in West Nashville was called Winn's Chapel. In 1926, the chapel was renamed Craig Memorial Methodist Church in honor of its pastor, Reverend Robert Craig. The church was located just off Charlotte Pike not far from the old railroad round house or New Shops.

During my childhood, when we visited my grandmother, I remember the pastor being referred to affectionately only as "Brother Craig." He often ate lunch at my grandmother's home after the Sunday church service. You may know the name, too. It was years later when I learned that Brother Craig was the father of Nashville's musician, band leader, and song writer Francis Craig.

There were and are many outstanding citizens of West Nashville. You remember J. Percy Priest who used to be on the editorial staff of *The Tennessean* newspaper. In 1940, he was elected as U. S. Congressman for the 5th district. Priest served until 1956.

Lewis E. Moore was our postmaster for many years. He retired in 1971. By the way, Lewis Moore served as the best man in Percy Priest's wedding.

Judge Bill Higgins and Judge Randall Wyatt are two former Cohn High School students who are presently serving as judges in Metro.

General James Robertson made his first residence near Richland Creek at 23rd and Park Avenue, west of James Avenue, and north of Robertson Road. The log house was recreated and now sits behind the West District police department in the H. G. Hill Park on Charlotte Pike. The Robertson's fine brick home named "Richland" was located at 5904 Robertson Road. The home burned in 1902.

There is a monument in Centennial Park dedicated to James Robertson. On Sunday afternoon, October 11, 1903, Robertson's descendants from 20 states and one foreign country gathered with the citizens of Nashville to unveil the Robertson Monument located on the edge of Lake Watauga in Centennial Park.

Many West Nashville youth spent a lot of time at Richland Park, the social center for kids of the era, located between the old Cohn High School building and Charlotte Pike. The park was so named for General James and Charlotte Robertson's home named "Richland."

In Richland Park kids could enjoy basketball courts, tennis courts, and softball fields. The park also had croquet courts and a swimming pool. During the summer months, free outdoor movies were shown in the park on Thursday nights. Miss Woolwine ran Richland Park and the Community Center with an iron hand. She probably weighed about 80 pounds soaking wet, but she ruled. No question about it!

West Nashville's old Elite Theatre opened in 1927 on Charlotte across from Richland Park by the Crescent Amusement Company with Tony Sudekum as owner and manager. There were two shows a day. A Seeburg organ played during the intermission. The aisles were covered with linoleum. A power projector was used on the full-size screen.

The theatre was torn down some years ago. The only time I was inside the old Elite was when I played on stage in an amateur contest. That was quite a few years ago.

The café next door to the theatre at one time was named Vance's. They served great hamburgers, wiener sandwiches, chili, and they had a candy counter.

Maybe many of you remember Doris's Drugstore on the corner of 46th and Charlotte which featured those much-loved chocolate sundaes and cherry cokes for a nickel.

There was a dinky [streetcar] that ran from Charlotte to Murphy Road on 46th Avenue. There was a horse watering trough located at 51st Avenue and Charlotte.

The great burger place back in the old days was Gables Drive-in Restaurant on Charlotte Pike.

Some of you may remember Holloran's Market and Lampley's Grocery located at 44th and Wyoming Avenue. My cousin, Murray Kennedy, had operated the same store for a time. Also, Floyd & Petty was another grocery which was sold in 1982, and became Brummitt's Cee Bee Grocery.

Have you had those good, home-cooked, meat and three meals, and that fabulous chocolate pie at the Sylvan Park Restaurant? Did you know that the Sylvan Park Restaurant was originally a pie wagon at 15th and West End? The restaurant moved to its present location on Murphy Road back in the early 1940s.

Many of you remember the old McConnell Air Field. You could take an airplane flight over Nashville for two dollars. It was operated by the Gasser Brothers.

In 1927, the city bought 131 acres of land and built the McConnell airport on the location which is now McCabe Park and Golf Course. It served as the Nashville Airport. It was named McConnell Field for Lieutenant Brower McConnell, a 30-year-old Tennessee National Guard pilot who died that year in an air crash while at Langley Field, Virginia.

The McConnell field was formerly a part of the Whitworth and Bosley farm. The old National Guard hangars were located about 50 yards east of the present McCabe Golf Course Clubhouse.

Aircraft outgrew the field in the 1930s and moved to Sky Harbor and Berry Field. In 1939, the park board built the McCabe Golf Course which still stands today at that West Nashville location.

Businessman Warren Sloan owned a farm in that area, and his home was located on the present site of the McCabe Park Community Center. Charles M. McCabe was a former Chairman of the Park Board.

Richland Park fell into decay by 1960. The old band shell and recreation center were converted into a library. Richland Park Branch Library was opened in October of 1961. The building was renovated and enlarged in 1979.

West Nashvillians can take great pride in the history of their New Town which we call West Nashville.

East Nashville's Pride Lives On

The early East Nashville was one of the loveliest areas in the South. "Edgefield" was a small satellite city of magnificent homes. Today, many Nashvillians are restoring some of those nice homes.

An early settler in Nashville was David Shelby. He bought a 640-acre piece of land from James Shaw who was considered to be the owner of much of East Nashville back in the early days.

Back in the 1800s, David Shelby presented this land as a Christmas gift to his sons John and Anthony. John Shelby bought Anthony's share for $2,500 and built himself a home on what is now Woodland Street between Second and Third Streets. He called his home "Shelby Hall."

Later, John Shelby built homes for his two daughters, Priscilla and Anna. These homes were called "Fatherland" and "Boscobel."

John Shelby was a physician and businessman. Also, he was the founder of Shelby Medical School in Nashville.

In addition to beautiful homes, businesses began to spring up in East Nashville. Some of you may remember some of the corner stores like Simpkins Grocery on Shelby Avenue, or pharmacies like Hoosers on Woodland Street, or Eastside on Fatherland Street. Many of these old stores operated up until the 1970s and 1980s.

I am sure former residents of East Nashville still hold fond memories of Sandersons, which later became the Fulton Five & Ten on Woodland Street. There were Powell Phillips' Esso Service Station, Mrs. Ashbough's Candy Shop, Vester's Billiards at the corner of Woodland and Eleventh, and many of us saw movies at the old Woodland Theatre.

Many should remember the J. W. Grimes Grocery at 16th and Woodland. It later housed the Nashville Photo Service.

Another grocery was the Lehning Brothers' Grocery at 1012 Woodland Street. That store operated until the mid-1980s. Lehning's was a grocery store, soda fountain, and candy shop.

Grocery stores back in the old days were not self-service stores. All of the merchandise was on shelves around the walls. A grocery clerk would write up your order, collect the items, make out a grocery ticket, and bag the goods for you to carry off.

Another fine home in East Nashville was called "Renraw." It was the home of James Warner, a businessman and manufacturer. James was the father of Percy Warner. Percy also lived in Renraw until he later moved to Belle Meade. Renraw, the name of their home, was Warner spelled backwards.

This home is significant because around the year 1918, Trevecca College took over this location. My wife's family lived on Trevecca Avenue adjacent to Renraw. My wife's father, T. C. Young, a city Board of Education member for many years, attended this school.

In 1930, Trevecca College moved out and classes met in homes and in the Nazarene Church building on Woodland Street. In the mid 1930s, the school moved to its present campus on Murfreesboro Road. Today, the old Trevecca College campus in East Nashville off of Gallatin Road is the location of the Nashville Auto Diesel College.

Some of the earliest churches in East Nashville were Edgefield Baptist Church, East End Methodist Church, Seventeenth Street Church of Christ, Woodland Presbyterian Church, St. Ann's Episcopal Church, and Tulip Street Methodist Church.

In the late 1800s, Meigs School served as the first public school for African-American students in East Nashville, and in 1886 became Nashville's first African-American high school.

Some other early established schools in East Nashville were Warner, Eastland, Bailey, and Lockland.

When the J. J. Keyes Stadium was built beside East Nashville High School, it was considered one of the finest high school stadiums in the South. The stadium was located off of McFerrin Avenue, sitting just below the side of the high school building. It was named for Professor J. J. Keyes who served as the first principal of the school. The stadium seated 5,500 with additional accommodations for even more people. It had modern dressing rooms, lockers, showers, rooms for officials, and office space.

Albert E. Hill, president of the City Board of Education, and Mayor Hilary Howse presided over the stadium dedication in 1932.

Sorrowfully, the old Keyes Stadium was torn down in 1987. The new Ross Elementary School was built in its place. Behind Ross School is a large area where some of the old stadium and football field was. We can still see some remnants of the old structure there including the landscaped hill and some concrete steps.

Shelby Park was a greatly admired part of East Nashville. The park had a full-size Dutch windmill which stood majestically atop Windmill Hill. The old windmill was said to have burned in the early 1940s, but the stone steps are still visible leading up to the hilltop on which it stood.

As a child, I climbed those steps many times to get to the top of the windmill to look out over the park with its lake, baseball diamonds, and Sycamore Lodge which sat down close to the Cumberland River.

Sycamore Lodge is gone too. I remember when our ninth grade teacher at Waverly-Belmont Junior High School took us to Shelby Park for a year-end party. In Sycamore Lodge, we played games and listened to records. The recording that sticks in my mind most prominently is "Deep Purple" played by Larry Clinton and His Orchestra.

Shelby Park had a wonderful swimming pool. Many nights the kids from my neighborhood would go swimming in this heated pool with beautiful underwater lighting.

In the park is Lake Sevier. I remember that fishing tournaments at the lake were very popular. I especially remember one sponsored by the Fraternal Order of Police for the enjoyment of the children.

At the edge of the lake was a fanciful boathouse designed of wood and concrete which looked like the front of a riverboat. We could rent paddle boats and canoes to take out on the lake.

There was always a spirit of pride and closeness within the residents of East Nashville. Today, it is not hard to meet an East Nashvillian or a former East Nashvillian in whom you can sense this remaining pride in the glory days of old East Nashville.

East Nashville High School Stadium, razed in 1987

North Nashville's Pride Lives On

When Old Nashville first began moving toward the south, the streets were named for trees, such as Cherry, Spruce, Oak, Mulberry, Elm, Chestnut, Laurel, Ash, etc. Cedar Street (Charlotte Avenue today) became an important business section in the Old Nashville.

As Nashville grew and prospered, the city began to spread toward the north, and the streets were named for presidents, such as Jefferson, Monroe, Buchanan, Adams, Jackson, Harrison, Van Buren, Garfield, etc.

North Nashville has always been a sanctuary for many of Nashville's prize possessions. Some of the institutions are still with us today.

For instance, Fisk University opened in 1866. The school was named in honor of Federal officer General Clinton Fisk, who played a great part in founding the institution.

George White is credited with establishing the world-renowned Fisk Jubilee Singers who literally toured around the world raising money for the school. Their travels included performing at the White House, in Europe, and before England's Queen Victoria.

With the money they raised, Jubilee Hall was built from 1873 to 1876, and took on the name for the Jubilee Singers. This building on Jefferson Street is still standing there today.

Hadley Park at the intersection of 28th Avenue, North and Centennial Boulevard was established in 1912. Both Hadley Park and Tennessee State University are located on lands remaining from the antebellum plantation of John Hadley.

Hadley was an owner of slaves at one time. Later, he donated land because of his desire to help families of the freed slaves. Hadley Park today serves the community well in offering concerts, shows, entertainment, and athletic events.

Tennessee A & I State College grew into our present Tennessee State University, and is becoming a major university in America. The school has trained many outstanding musicians who have become nationally known. In addition, athletes have brought fame to the school. Many football players from TSU have filled important positions in the National Football League. I can recall Richard Dent, Too Tall Jones who played with the Dallas Cowboys, and Junior Gilliam who was a quarterback for the Pittsburgh Steelers, to name only a few.

Through the professionalism of Coach Ed Temple, we have seen many of his lady athletes qualify and perform in the Olympics. The great achievements of Wilma Rudolph and the well-trained Tigerbelles have brought glory to Nashville. Also, broad-jump star Ralph Boston was an Olympic Gold Medal winner in 1960.

In addition, many professors in academics have received honors and grants for exceptional study and work in academia.

Meharry Medical College was established in 1876, and has trained more African-American dentists, physicians, and surgeons than any other medical institution. Today, the College educates doctors of all races. And, a past Surgeon General for the United States, Dr. David Satcher, is a former Meharry president.

The Dominican Sisters reside in one of the most beautiful and historic structures in Nashville. The St. Cecilia Mother House and Novitiae since the mid-1800s sits on a secluded rise by Interstate 65 and Metro Center Boulevard just north of downtown Nashville.

Old North Nashville High School is gone, but talk to any graduates from North High, and they will convince you of their love for that old school.

The Farmer's Market has been through many transitions, but we still have it. My understanding is that back in 1912, Nashville had a Farmer's Market located around the Courthouse on the Public Square.

Around 1954, the Farmer's Market was situated around Sixth Avenue North and Jackson Street. Then, in 1995 it moved into the new facility located adjacent to the Bi-Centennial Mall north of our state capitol building.

In that same general area was the old Nashville Stockyards. They are no longer there. A portion of the establishment was renovated to become the Stockyards Restaurant.

Sulphur Dell baseball park was for many years located at Fifth Avenue, North roughly in the vicinity of the Bi-Centennial Mall. In 1963, when the last baseball game was played at Sulphur Dell, it was noted as being the oldest baseball park in America.

Werthen Bag Company on Eighth Avenue, North for many years was not only a successful business, but its owners were the benefactors which brought great assistance to our citizens in Nashville, in our state, and in our entire country.

Morgan Park had the sulphur spring water. We used to be able to drink sulphur water right from the park fountains, as well as fill our jugs to take home.

There is some interesting history concerning a public school in what is called Germantown. In 1865, the Ninth Ward School was established on rented property in an old Army house erected on the lot at the corner of Madison and North Cherry Street (Fourth Avenue, North.)

In 1872, a lot was purchased at the corner of North High Street (Sixth Avenue, North) and Jefferson Street, and the ninth ward Elliott School was built.

The present building was built in 1916. It was last used as a Metro School building in 1971. It served as a daycare center from 1972 until 1976 and soon became vacant. In 1989, a group of Germantown residents purchased the historic school.

In May of 1995, the school was converted to the Ella Bullard Hayes Center for Children and Adolescents. Excellent work is done there with students who have emotional and behavioral problems. So, good came from an old school which had its beginnings way back in Germantown in the late 1800s.

North Nashvillians have much for which they can take pride.

South Nashville's Pride Lives On

Maybe the most interesting thing about South Nashville, is that many of the old things of by-gone days are still there.

Other sections of Nashville have experienced many changes. Downtown Nashville is almost in a constant change syndrome.

There are some things in South Nashville which are still present after the passing of many years, such as Rutledge Hill, Radnor Yards, Radnor Lake, the Fairgrounds, the reservoir, remnants of Fort Negley, the old City Cemetery, Sunnyside Mansion in Sevier Park, the Battle of Nashville monument, and more.

The State Fairgrounds have some of the same qualities today as were present in the distant past. The grandstand and some exhibition buildings burned back in 1965, but what was replaced for those structures still stand. The same nostalgic experience is felt when we enter the fairgrounds from Wedgewood Avenue, drive up the hill, and go through the tunnel and find ourselves right where the old grandstand sat for us to watch the free acts, the harness races, and the fireworks.

The old water reservoir on Eighth Avenue, South still sits majestically upon the hill from where it has served the city for many years,

A little closer to downtown are the remnants of old Fort Negley. This fort was built beginning in 1862 by the Federal Army. The remnants of the old fort are still there since the Civil War. The fort is located on Saint Cloud Hill behind Greer Stadium off of Eighth Avenue, South.

I am reminded of an incident about these two South Nashville historical structures in our city.

When I was active in the Boy Scouts as a youngster, I became rather proficient in signaling codes, both the International Morse Code and the Semaphore Code. Through Semaphore Code, we sent messages by the use of flags.

On a Saturday morning many years ago, our Boy Scout Patrol Leader, Billy Wright, took a group of us kids up to old Fort Negley. Then, our Patrol Leader went over to a high point at the reservoir in Reservoir Park. We were to send Semaphore messages back and forth.

We spent a good bit of time enjoying each other's messages. Finally, in our haste, we wrote down our Patrol Leader's final message. We wrote, "I am going here. You too."

We thought that he meant that he was coming back to where we were. We waited, and we waited. As it began to get darker and darker, we decided we should walk back to our Patrol Leader's house on Beechwood Avenue. When we got there and inquired, he said, "No, no, my message was, 'I am going home. You too.'" We got the message except for two little letters! So much for proficiency!

I have written about the presence of Rutledge Hill, and the old fort-like building which still stands from the old University of Nashville. Still there!

The old General Hospital building which opened in 1890 is still there in all of its ancient splendor over-looking the banks of the Cumberland River. True, the hospital has relocated to Hubbard Hospital and Meharry Medical College. But, the old General Hospital building is still there on Hermitage Avenue.

The old tunnel on Thompson Lane under the railroad tracks is still there. It has been enlarged, but it is still there. When we were kids, we had our parents sound the auto horn as we got to the middle of that old narrow tunnel. Every car that went through the tunnel blew the horn to hear that reverberation.

Becker's Bakery is still at the corner of 12th Avenue, South and Montrose Avenue. That bakery was established in 1925. The same building is still there, and they still make the same raisin sweet rolls from the same recipe which my father used to bring home to us back in the 1930s.

The Old City Cemetery is still at Oak Street and Fourth Avenue, South since 1822. It brings Old Nashville much clearer and nearer in our minds when we know the many historical figures buried there.

Noted Nashvillian John Overton's home called Traveller's Rest still sits in South Nashville since the first section of it was built in 1799. Overton's home is a classic example of an early aristocratic Tennessee farmhouse.

Many of the important structures of Old South Nashville still remain in place, but some things have faded away. For instance, the old Hay Market is gone. It was one city block between Third and Fourth Avenues south of Broadway. Farmers from all over drove their horse and mule wagons full of farm products to market at the old Hay Market. They did a lot of selling and swapping of horses, mules, and cows. It was called the Hay Market because of all the hay there to feed the animals.

When I was in the Army ROTC (Reserved Officers Training Corps) at Hume-Fogg High School (1939-1940), we marched down to the Hay Market location each morning where we would have enough room to drill.

The first streetcar pulled by mules ran out the South Nashville line in 1866. Later, streetcars were powered by electricity. Also, I read where the old Fairfield streetcars carried people out to Mt. Olivet and Mt. Calvary cemeteries in the old days.

The old Tennessee School for the Blind was created in 1843 by a man named James Chaplin. Back then it was just a small school. Later, the facility became a state school funded by the Tennessee Department of Education.

In 1853, a new school building was constructed on Lebanon Pike in an area which we now call Donelson. Later, Nashvillian John M. Lea bought the old Claiborne mansion on Fillmore Street which is now called Hermitage Avenue. Lea donated the property to the state for the school, and the Tennessee School for the Blind stayed there for almost 80 years.

In 1952, the fine school was moved to its present location at 115 Stewarts Ferry Pike off of Lebanon Pike.

The Tennessee Central railroad crossing on the old Lebanon Road was the Nashville city limits in the old days before Metro government took in the entire Davidson County. Where I lived as a boy, the TC railroad crossing over Belmont Boulevard at Gale Lane was the boundary of the old city limits there. I sometimes used to walk those railroad tracks from near West End High School to

Belmont Boulevard, and then on home. The tracks are gone. Interstate 440 passes through that area now.

Some of you real South Nashville old-timers may remember Ike Karnarsky's store, Kleiser's Drugstore, Booth Furniture Store, and the horse water trough on Chestnut Street.

Central High School used to sit where the public television station sits today on Rains Avenue near the Fairgrounds. The old Central High football stadium was located at the corner of Rains and Wedgewood Avenues.

The old Fairgrounds Coliseum burned down around 1970 and was never rebuilt. That is where we musicians used to play the Shrine Circus and the horse shows. During the Tennessee State Fair of old, there was a horse show in the Coliseum every night during fair week.

Gone is the old Cascade Plunge swimming pool which was located within the fairgrounds close to Nolensville Road. Gone is the old bell gate of Mt. Olivet Cemetery. Glendale Park and the Glendale Park Zoo are gone.

Today, we have the wonderful Adventure Science Museum (which used to be called Cumberland Science Museum) located at 800 Fort Negley Boulevard.

The Battle of Nashville monument is not gone, but it has been moved. For many years, this old marble and bronze monument sat at the west end of Thompson Lane right at Franklin Pike.

When Interstates and other roads were being built or altered, this Battle of Nashville monument was in a location where it could hardly be seen. For a while, a fence was built around the monument to try and keep it from being damaged.

Finally, the monument was moved to its present location at the corner of Granny White Pike and Battlefield Drive.

In the old days, we had a school called TIS. It stood for Tennessee Industrial School. It helped children from broken and disturbed homes.

Later, the name of the school on Foster Avenue in South Nashville was changed to TPS, which stands for Tennessee Preparatory School. TPS was a well-run school, and offered help to children in need.

The school had a football team, and I remember when I was the band director at Hillsboro High School, our football team played TPS. I took the Hillsboro Band to a game there one Friday night in the 1950s.

Now, a plan has been set in place to either alter the present school arrangement, or close it. I hope and pray that the change will be for the good of the students.

Yes, many things have remained the same in old South Nashville, and there have been some changes, too. South Nashville offers a lot to our city, and old South Nashvillians still beam with their deserved pride.

North Nashville High School

University of Nashville

Special Days of the Year

Today is the first day of the rest of your life!

Thompson grandchildren celebrating Thanksgiving –
Kevin (standing), Kelly, Katy, and Kimberly Parsley

New Year's Day

New Years in All Generations

New Year's Day is like going out of the woods!

You know the old riddle which asks, "How far can you go into the woods?" You know the answer, "You can go only half way, and then you are going out."

New Year's Day is like going out of the past, and going into the future. Beginning a New Year is like getting a second chance. It's a chance to try harder to do things better.

Thinking back in history: In the Middle Ages, New Year's Day was celebrated among Christians usually on March 25. After the adoption of the Gregorian calendar, replacing the old Roman calendar, New Year's Day was observed on the first day of January.

The Jewish New Year is the first day of Tishri, which falls some time in September or in early October.

The Chinese New Year (between January 10 and February 19 of the Gregorian calendar) is considered the most important of their festivals.

The Muslim New Year falls on the first day of Muharram.

I can let my mind drift back to when I was a kid. I can remember one New Year's Day in particular. My sister and I were lying on the living room floor in front of our old Majestic radio listening to the Rose Bowl football game from Pasadena, California. To be exact, the year was 1931 and Alabama was playing Washington State. Alabama won 24 to 0.

While listening to the game, our mother made us a huge cookie, and I remember that we broke it into six pieces so it would last a long time. Now, every time I hear the excitement of a football bowl game on the radio or television, I have real warm feelings of that past time. My mind even recaptures the smell coming from the kitchen.

As a musician all of my life, I enjoy remembering the many New Year's Eve dinner-dances that I played in bands over the years.

I can remember the first one that I played in a big band. It was on December 31, 1942. I played at the Old Hickory Country Club with Horace Holley and His Orchestra.

I remember playing with some great orchestras on New Year's Eve at the Opryland Hotel, Hermitage Hotel, Belle Meade Country Club, Colemere Country Club, Richland Country Club, and other places.

When my children were young, I recall that I always picked up two balloons and two New Year's Eve hats when the dance was over. My children expected them. And, on New Year's Day, we ate our meals with my son and daughter wearing their hats. My wife and I too would find something to wear on our heads in celebration. I have some good memories.

On New Year's Day, we would sit by the log fire, watch the football bowl games, eat black-eyed peas, and enjoy being together. If we were really blessed, there might be a little snow drifting down which lined the tree branches in white giving the winter's effect of a Christmas picture postcard.

For many people, a New Year is a new beginning. Old things are cast away. Thousands of New Year's resolutions are made at the beginning of a new year. Many resolutions are broken each year. But, the fact that we make resolutions and set goals means that we are aware of the need for changes and progress in our lives. That's a start.

Another way to start a New Year is to give praise. "Lord, thou hast been our dwelling place in all generations." (Psalms 90:1 KJV)

Valentine's Day

Won't You Be My Valentine?

Is Valentine's Day as big now as it used to be?

I can remember all of us school kids buying an inexpensive box of valentines, and giving one to each student in our class. On some valentines we would just sign our name. On others, where there was a little desire to do something special, we would write a short statement or draw a heart, and then sign our name.

Some years we would make our own valentines out of paper doilies, red paper, wallpaper samples, and pictures cut out of magazines. The teacher would have us decorate a big valentine box. We would place all of our valentines in the box, and distribute them to all of the students.

Many high schools organized and held Valentine dances on the weekend. I remember being invited to a Valentine dance at Hillsboro High School during the very first year the school was built. Also, I remember the Valentine dances at West End High School where I was a student.

Being a musician all of my life, I played many Valentine dinner-dances. I can remember the last one that I played. It was at the Hillwood Country Club. There were nice decorations, a photographer took pictures, and a wonderful dinner was served.

Another yearly Valentine celebration was held at the old Ward-Belmont College. Each year the students celebrated Valentine's Day as the King and Queen of Hearts marched through the dining room to their throne to reign over the Valentine festivities. The students put up the decorations, and arranged the musical program for the formal dinner.

I think celebrating Valentine's Day is great. Taking a special day to tell your wife, husband, or sweetheart that you love them might start a trend. Who knows!

Be my Valentine, readers of *Westview*,
As we dispense some enjoyment to you.
Keep a nostalgic love for the old Nashville way,
But, be my Valentine on this new Valentine's Day.

The Nashville Knights

Easter

Happy in Your Easter Bonnet

By the way, how do you know which Sunday to celebrate Easter?

Christians observe Easter on the first Sunday following the first full moon after the vernal equinox which is the first day of Spring in the Northern Hemisphere. Therefore, the celebration of Easter can occur on any Sunday between March 22 and April 25.

Easter nostalgia goes way back in my memories. I served as a choir director in churches for 30 years. My whole family served with me. You can imagine how much music and how many special Palm Sunday, Maundy Thursday, Good Friday, Tenebrae, and Easter services we prepared in years gone by.

My wife, Sonia, was beside me for the entire 30 years. She served in many different capacities over the years including singer, soloist, robe caretaker, music librarian, children's choir director, co-director of youth choir, singer in recording sessions, and much revered public relations specialist in spreading love and a caring attitude to everyone.

Our son, Jeff, experienced the music ministry from children's choirs, to youth choir, to playing clarinet in the orchestra, to writing and performing puppet shows for the children's choirs, to finally being a very strong bass in the adult choir and on recording sessions.

Our daughter, Lee Anne, sang almost before she walked. She even experienced an extra year in the first grade choir. She started a year early while in kindergarten since her mother was the director of that first grade choir. She had to sit somewhere during rehearsal!

Lee Anne went on to serve in the children, youth, and adult choirs as well as perform on recording sessions.

Easter is associated with the season of Spring. The new plant life that comes out in Spring symbolizes the new life that Christians gain because of the crucifixion and resurrection of Jesus Christ.

My nostalgic memories go back even to when I was a child. No matter how poor any of us were during The Great Depression, it was our duty and our goal to have something new to wear to church on Easter. Everyone made their way to church with a new shirt, dress, hat, or maybe a half-soled pair of shoes which had been polished to the brilliance of a mirror.

Most ladies wore hats to church back when I was a child, but on Easter we could expect to see some really nice, new hats on many of the ladies in the congregation. Irving Berlin's song, "Easter Parade," even mentions, "In your Easter bonnet with all the frills upon it..."

I can remember two or three Easter Sundays on which it snowed in Nashville. My wife reminded me of when she was about eleven or twelve. She had a nice, new Easter dress, some nice shoes, and a new hat.

When everyone sprang out of bed on that Easter Sunday, our eyes saw the sight of snow covering the ground. My wife's mother wouldn't let her wear her beautiful new dress and new shoes to church in that damp, slushy, messy weather. But, my wife said that she did wear her new hat which she dearly loved. It probably didn't register fashionable with the old dress and old shoes that she wore, however.

Many churches did and still celebrate outdoor Easter services at sunrise. I can remember some very beautiful ones. Outdoors with the Tennessee hills as the backdrop make for a very memorable and spiritual experience.

Also, I remember that Easter morning used to be the time for the members of the new confirmation class in church to come to the altar during the worship service and join the church. I remember mine well.

I was twelve years old when I joined the church. My family had joined the old Waverly Place Methodist Church on 10th Avenue, South, across the street from Waverly-Belmont Junior High School which I attended. That was my first church. Also, that was the church which sponsored my Boy Scout Troop 26.

Today, that old church building still stands there on the corner of 10th Avenue and Caruthers Avenue, but it is now occupied by another church congregation. Now, it is the home of the Greater Christ Temple.

Since my childhood, old Waverly Place Methodist Church moved out to Old Hickory Boulevard in Brentwood, and the church was renamed Forest Hills United Methodist Church.

We have been there many times to visit, and there are still some of the old Waverly Place members there. They are in their seventies and eighties, and I love every one of them.

I naturally have to speak from the standpoint of a member of the Christian faith, but I wish for everyone a Happy Easter and a wonderful Spring day on this next Easter Sunday.

May Day

The New Life of Spring

May Day! No, I am not thinking of the international radio signal used as a distress call. I am thinking of happiness here! I am thinking of a Springtime festival.

May Days in our past brought a great deal of happiness. When we heard the words "May Day," it meant that the dreary days of the snow, cold, dampness had departed and turned our city into a Springtime playground. May Day marked the revival of life in a Nashville Spring.

I remember the Spring bathing of warm weather brightening up our lives. At school we looked forward to May Day when many track and field events were held outside.

We had good teacher leadership in setting up relay races, the 50 and 100-yard dashes, the high jump, the broad jump, the three-legged race, and leap-frog races. Also, we had marble tournaments.

I always enjoyed the tug of war. I always tried to get on the team with the biggest boys so we could pull that rope right across the field and impress the girls.

A May Day celebration was a big tradition at the old Ward-Belmont College. This was an annual production on their campus stretching from majestic Acklen Hall into the grassy area amidst the white-pillared buildings of the central campus.

Each year many Nashvillians went to the campus to attend the festivities.

Ward-Belmont College was considered one of the finest finishing schools for girls in the country. The students learned all of the social graces, music, art, ballet, and everything which taught them to become acceptable, well-cultured young ladies in any situation.

On May Day, I remember the backdrop of magnolias on campus, the fluttering ribbons on the maypoles, the colorful folk dances, the gorgeous dresses, and the procession of the May Queen and her attendants in their horse-drawn royal coaches.

The dance around the maypole involved the ladies holding the ends of colorful ribbons that streamed from the top of the pole. They wove the ribbons around the pole until the pole was covered with bright colors.

I had the honor of playing in the orchestra for one of the last May Day celebrations at Ward-Belmont College. Some of us from the Nashville Symphony played for the Festival while seated in the gazebo on campus. The conductor was Harold Johnson who was the concertmaster of the Symphony back then. Harold also played violin in the staff orchestra at WSM radio.

The Southern Baptist Convention purchased the college, and opened Belmont College (now Belmont University) in 1951 as a four-year co-ed college.

If you know of another school which presents a May Day Festival, be sure to attend. You will enjoy the happiness and enthusiasm from the students and teachers. And, you will feel the new life of Spring.

Mother's Day

Let's Wish for Roses at the Steeplechase

It is easy for me to remember when the Iroquois Memorial Steeplechase is held in our city, and when Mother's Day comes.

The Kentucky Derby is run on the first Saturday in May. The Iroquois is run on the second Saturday in May. Mother's Day is on the second Sunday in May.

Now, it doesn't have to happen every year, but most often the Steeplechase is on the day before Mother's Day, because the second Saturday in May and the second Sunday in May occur side by side on the calendar in most years. Easy for me to remember!

I remember when the Iroquois Steeplechase was built in Percy Warner Park. I attended the first race. The year was 1941. We parked our car in the open field across Old Hickory Boulevard.

That field is now the Bob Heriges Memorial Baseball Field. The field is in memory of sportsman and athlete Robert M. Heriges who lived from 1921 until 1967.

There were no seats for the races back then. Spectators just spread a blanket and sat on the side of the hill.

Our Steeplechase is well respected nationally, and the profits go to charity.

Iroquois was the first American bred horse ever to have won the English Derby. It was back in 1881. Iroquois was retired to stud at the Belle Meade Plantation where the horse is also buried. The Steeplechase was named for the horse Iroquois. Belle Meade developed into one of the world's great thoroughbred horse farms. Our present day Harding Road is named for the Harding family.

I have memories of the Hunt Ball which used to be held on the Saturday night following the afternoon races. For eleven years, following the Saturday Steeplechase, I played the Hunt Ball at the Belle Meade Country Club with an orchestra from West Palm Beach, Florida. It was the Cliff Hall Orchestra which was well known all over the East Coast and beyond. After Cliff died, his fine clarinet player and vocalist, Neal Smith, took over the band. I got to work with Neal at one of the Swan Balls at Cheekwood as well as eleven of the Hunt Balls.

Following most of those Balls, I remember that the next day was Mother's Day. My family went to church and wore our white or red carnations or roses. That tradition was around when I was a child. In our backyard, we had several rose bushes, both white and red.

The tradition was that on Mother's Day everyone wore a red rose to church if their mother was still alive. For those whose mothers had passed away, they honored them by wearing a white rose.

I remember one year when our red roses in the backyard didn't fill out very well. Somewhere, my mother found a pink rose for me to wear. I said, "This rose isn't red. It's half white." My mother laughed and said, "That's O. K. I'm about half dead anyway." That's a joke, son!

We don't have any rose bushes at our present home in Bellevue. If they have a bunch of roses at the Steeplechase, maybe we can get a couple from there to wear to church this Sunday for Mother's Day..

If you can, tell your mother how much you love her. It will be a whole year before you can celebrate that day again.

Memorial Day

Honoring War's Fallen

Do you remember that Memorial Day used to be called Decoration Day? After World War I, families honored and placed flowers on the graves of those fallen during the war. Later, the name of the day was changed to Memorial Day to honor all men and women who died in all of the wars.

For many years in the past, I played in the Post 5 American Legion Band on Memorial Day out at the Nashville National Military Cemetery off of Gallatin Road.

In more recent years, Memorial Day has been observed at two locations. When the newer state owned Middle Tennessee Veterans Cemetery was opened on McCrory Lane off of Interstate 40 near Pegram, the American Legion began to hold two separate ceremonies at the two locations on two different days to commemorate Memorial Day. Our community seems to hold a great interest in honoring our fallen military men and women from the wars.

When I was active in the Boy Scouts back in the late 1930s and early 1940s, I received quite a number of merit badges leading to my Eagle Scout award. Being interested in music, I naturally had to get the music and bugler's merit badges.

We had a good bugler at old Camp Boxwell down on the Harpeth River near The Narrows. Everyone was familiar with the "reveille" call. We could sing words to it: "You've got to get up, you've got to get up, you've got to get up this morning."

We knew "chow" [meal] call because we could sing the words "Soupy, soupy, soupy" with the correct notes to it.

"Assembly" was a good bugle call. And, every evening during camp, we went out and fell in formation around the flag pole to have the flag lowering ceremony accompanied by the "retreat" bugle call.

At night, when we heard "TAPS," we knew that there could be no more talk or noise of any kind in the tents.

Everyone knows the mournful cry of TAPS which is played at the end of the camp's day, but mainly as a respectful farewell to a fallen military person.

When we observe Memorial Day and honor all of the fallen service men and women, we shall hear the bugler's mournful sound of TAPS.

There is an interesting story passed down through the years from the days of the Civil War.

In 1862, Union Army Captain Robert Ellicombe was stationed in Virginia with his men. The Confederate Army was located on a strip of land near by.

During the night, Captain Ellicombe heard the cries of a wounded soldier lying out on the battlefield. Not caring whether it was a Union or a Confederate soldier, Ellicombe decided to try and save the man's life.

Upon reaching the stricken soldier, Captain Ellicombe began pulling him back toward his encampment. When he got him there, he realized that he was a Confederate soldier, and he was dead.

Then, Captain Ellicombe lit a lantern, looked at the soldier, and was thrust into great anguish as he looked upon the face of his own son dead in his arms.

Captain Ellicombe's son had been studying music in the South when the war broke out. The young man had enlisted in the Confederate Army.

The next morning, this grief-stricken father asked permission of his superiors to give his son a full military burial.

Captain Ellicombe's request was to have the Army band play a funeral dirge for his son. His request was turned down because the soldier was a Confederate. However, out of respect for the good captain, his superiors allowed him to choose one musician. Captain Ellicombe chose a bugler.

Captain Ellicombe asked the bugler to play a series of musical notes he had found on a piece of paper in the pocket of his dead son's uniform.

Those notes of music have become the renowned, haunting, and familiar melody we now know as TAPS.

Father's Day

Remembering Father's Day

On Father's Day, don't forget, it's the little things that matter!

I remember when I was about ten years old, Daddy and I would get up very early in the morning to go fishing at Radnor Lake. Early in the morning was when the fish would bite according to my daddy.

Back when I was a child, we thought of Radnor Lake as being "out in the country" on the south edge of Davidson County. To get to the lake, we went straight out Granny White Pike from Nashville. I remember that we passed the site of where Lucinda "Granny" White's cabin stood. She was a legendary inn-keeper in the early 1800s. We turned left onto Otter Creek Road, and came upon a pictorial sight of water amidst the thick woods.

Back in those days, Radnor Lake was owned by the L & N (Louisville and Nashville) railroad company. This man-made 85-acre lake served as a water supply for the steam engines operating at the nearby Radnor Yards located off of Franklin Pike.

My father was a railroader for many years before his death. Being an employee, all he had to do was ask for a permit to go fishing in Radnor Lake.

While sitting with my daddy at the lake early in the morning, I can recall the quiet, misty haze lingering on the water. We would be quiet and hear the birds. We could see the multi-colored wildflowers. We could smell the woods, and hear the trees swaying in the gentle breeze. We could gaze upon the hills and water, and be in awe at the Creator's painting of the wide open spaces.

All we needed to go fishing was the permit, a cane pole, a string line, a cork to float on the water, a small rock to tie on the line for a sinker, a safety pin for a hook, and a worm from the ground. Don't laugh! We caught fish during The Great Depression!

Even today, many years later, I can stand on Otter Creek Road and look at that same bank where Daddy and I used to sit in the early morning while waiting for the fish to bite.

My daddy, who died in 1941, would never believe all of the changes we have seen in and around Nashville.

On Father's Day, don't fail to tell your father that you love him. If he has passed on, don't worry, he still might hear your words. But, more importantly, you will feel and experience the words you mean.

Independence Day

4th of July: Independence Day, and More!

What did you do in the good old summertime to celebrate the 4th of July? I can recall picnics, playing ball, going swimming, eating watermelon, and concerts in the park.

The old band shell in Centennial Park offered many concerts. I remember Leon Cole who played organ programs. Sometimes plays were presented. And, when the sun went down, good movies were shown for free. Some of the very same events continue today.

Later, when I became a musician, I guess I played a thousand concerts from the band shell in Centennial Park. I remember playing programs with different local dance bands and concert bands. Also, I played concerts there with the Nashville Symphony Orchestra.

I remember during some part of the 4th of July holiday period, we would go to town and eat at Varallo's on Church Street located between Eighth and Ninth Avenues. I would always order a bowl of chili-three-ways. That was made up of chili, spaghetti, and tamales. Another way it was three-ways was delicious, delightful, and delectable!

Varallo's on Church Street closed its doors on December 30, 1998. My wife and I went to town on that day, gladly stood in line, and got our final bowl of chili-three-ways on the last day before that great old restaurant closed its doors. The building was torn down, and today cars are using the space as a parking lot.

On some 4th of July holidays, a bunch of us would go to Cascade Plunge for swimming. Or, if we had some transportation, we would go to Willow Plunge in Franklin. Both swimming pools are things of the past.

I am sure there were some of the holidays when we went to a movie. In the neighborhoods, we might have gone to the Belmont Theatre at the corner of Twenty-First and Blakemore Avenues. The Educator's Credit Union is located today at that rebuilt corner location.

Or, we might have gone over to the Melrose Theatre on Franklin Road. The old Melrose Theatre building is now occupied by Scene Three, a company which tapes videos and commercials.

Or, sometimes we may have gone to the Belle Meade Theatre on Harding Road. All three of those theatres are now gone; however, we can still walk into the old Belle Meade Theatre which is now the home of Bookstar bookstore.

We still can see many photos in the lobby that the theatre manager, Mr. E. J. Jordan, collected over the years from movie stars who had visited the theatre. Many of us remember the old Happiness Club on Saturdays at the Belle Meade that Mr. Jordan hosted.

The old Peabody College used to have big summer sessions when teachers from all over the country would come in for additional study. Every 4th of July, the college lawn was covered with tables on which watermelons for all of the students would be cut and served by the college faculty. The faculty would garb themselves in aprons, chef hats, and, with large knives, cut the melons and serve the students.

There is one special 4th of July which I remember. The year was 1971. Our family was out driving, and the kids wanted to stop by the animal shelter on Harding Place just a block or so off of Harding Road.

As we looked at the animals, we saw a small, brown puppy whose sweet, little face made us fall in love with him. We paid for the puppy to get his shots, and we took him home.

Because it was the 4th of July, we immediately named our puppy Sammy for Uncle Sam. Our children knew the meaning of the 4th of July, Independence Day, respect for the American flag, and the love and patriotism we have for our country.

Our daughter, Lee Anne, was five years old, and our son, Jeff, was twelve. Talk about two thrilled kids!

In fact, I guess I was about as excited as the kids. But, my wife, Sonia, didn't want to generate near as much excitement as the rest of us.

But, that evening, who was it that wanted to give the puppy some warm milk, put him on a pallet, and keep him in the playroom the first night so he wouldn't cry?

We were able to keep our Sammy for a good many years before his death. We always missed Sammy after that. Even my memories today are of him running around me in the yard when I cut the grass. I can see the picture in my mind of Sammy running along behind Lee Anne's bicycle.

I remember the 8mm home movie we took of Lee Anne when she got her new red dress which was appropriate to wear on the 4th of July, and Sammy was seen running in the background. He was so happy that all of us were together out in the yard.

The classic movie shot was when Jeff put Sammy in his red wagon and pulled him around the yard. Sammy put one foot up on the side of the wagon, and with dignity, held his head up high.

Most nostalgia makes me happy when I reminisce. But, some nostalgia simply reminds me that we should live each day of our lives doing things to make people happy and things of which we can be proud.

We need to leave a legacy of love for God, our family, our country, and all human beings. Time moves too swiftly which can make us lose some great opportunities.

September 11, 2001

Dear Joe Revisited

All of us remember December 7, 1941 as "the date that will live in infamy" when the Japanese attacked Pearl Harbor. In this generation, all of us shall remember the event we call "911." This was the terrorists' attack on our country--the bombing of the New York World Trade Center buildings, the Pentagon in Washington, and the crash of the high-jacked plane in Pennsylvania.

Let me take you back to the attitude of patriotism and the unity of Americanism that existed in that other era from my generation of what we call "The War Years."

William Henry Oliver served as the principal of old East Nashville High School for many years. During those war years, Professor Oliver made a point to write letters to all of the East High students who were serving in the Armed Forces. Then, at the close of World War II, Professor Oliver put his letters in a small book which he gave the title *Dear Joe*.

The "Foreword" to his book was written by Nancy Gossage who was the editor of East High's *Eagle* Newspaper in 1945-46.

My wife, a graduate of East High, brought this little book out the other day, and I was interested in the first paragraph of the "Foreword."

The exact words of that paragraph from the "Foreword" of Professor Oliver's book written after the attack on Pearl Harbor could easily have been written concerning the calamitous day of September 11, 2001 in America's history. The paragraph states:

"Immediately after the fateful day of December 7, 1941, the military, economic, educational, political, social, religious, and moral life of the United States underwent many far-reaching changes."

That statement could have been written sixty years later about this September 11th event, the event which we refer to as "911." There are many similarities between these two events of 1941 and 2001.

For both happenings, the military guards were dispatched to watch airports, train stations, reservoirs, water treatment plants, power plants, and TVA dams and locks.

At the beginning of World War II, I was playing on live radio shows at WLAC in 1941. One morning I found a locked gate leading into the broadcast studios and control room. Communications had to be protected from an enemy take-over or a possibility of sabotage.

For the recent "911" happening, Mayor Rudy Giuliani of New York City took leadership in his city and asked the people to stay calm as he went about his work doing positive things.

Back in 1941, New York's Fiorello LaGuardia, in his role of mayor as well as head of the National Office of Civilian Defense, asked the citizens to stay calm and not panic.

My sister, Elva, with her young son, Jim, was living in New York City during World War II when her husband, Major James E. Fitzwater, was serving as a medical officer on the Queen Mary which was being used as a hospital ship. My sister told me that during that time, New York's Mayor LaGuardia even read the "funny paper" over the radio to the children to offer help in calming their lives.

The attack on Pearl Harbor lasted just under two hours. More than 2,400 United States military personnel and civilians died, and another 1,178 were wounded. Nineteen United States ships were sunk, capsized or damaged.

On the September 11, 2001 attack by terrorists, the 110-story twin towers of the World Trade Center in New York were demolished, other buildings were destroyed or damaged, thousands of innocent citizens from more than 80 different countries were killed, many others were wounded, and untold additional damages were thrust upon our country and its citizens.

Let's honor the many families who saw loved ones serve to protect our freedom in past years.

Also, let's pray for the many families suffering today around the world, and honor the men and women who are serving our country today to defend freedom.

Veterans' Day

Our Country

On November 11th each year, our country celebrates what we now call Veterans' Day. This day salutes all of the veterans that served their country in all of the wars.

Back when I was a child, November 11th was called Armistice Day. The armistice terminated World War I on November 11, 1918.

As a child in the 1930s, I remember standing with my family on Capitol Boulevard watching the Armistice Day parade go by. I was very impressed with what I saw.

Across the street from where we stood was the Knickerbocker Theatre. To my right on Church Street at the foot of Capitol Boulevard stood the Loew's Vendome Theatre. And, up the street to my left, I could see the Tennessee State Capitol building with the American and the Tennessee flags flying at great height in all their glory.

I recall seeing World War I veterans marching in the parade. Some wore their old uniforms. Some men made the war vivid in our minds by wearing mud splattered uniforms representing their duty when lying in the trenches of France while defending our country.

I was impressed to see all of the spectators on the sidelines either salute the American flag, or place their right hand directly over their heart when the American flag passed by them in the parade.

Many years later, I too was a veteran, but a veteran of World War II. I too marched in the parades. In my case, I marched and played in the American Legion Post 5 Band with many of my friends.

In 1954, Armistice Day changed its name and was given the official title of Veterans' Day. On this day, I salute my country and all of its veterans. Patriotism in our country has always meant a lot.

Patriotism is the love and loyal support of one's country. Patriotism can be displayed in the literature, art, and music of countries.

Through the study of history, citizens learn to love their country and admire its heroes. Patriotism is manifested in symbols such as flags, songs, national shrines, and monuments.

Patriotism requires public service and responsibilities of all citizens. President John F. Kennedy stated in his inaugural address of 1961, "Ask not what your country can do for you--ask what you can do for your country."

The word patriotism comes from the Greek word patris which means homeland. On Veterans' Day, I salute my homeland, and I pray that she will always stand for what is good and right.

John F. Kennedy's Assassination

Where Were You on November 22, 1963?

Everyone I have ever talked to, remembers exactly where they were on that infamous day when President John F. Kennedy was assassinated. I am no exception.

I was enrolled at George Peabody College for the 1963-64 school year working on a graduate degree in music. When this grave announcement about the shooting interrupted all television and radio programs, I was in the music library on the second floor of the Social-Religious Building at Peabody.

This quiet library, where many of us were studying or employing the old-time method of looking up books from the card catalog, was interrupted when a student ran into the library screaming that the president had been shot.

I was a music major, but for a moment, my life turned quickly into a psychology and sociology major. For the next fast, furious, and brain draining, sorrowful hour, I studied all of the people around me and how they reacted as each of us stood there in sorrow and confusion.

I saw some girls begin to cry. I saw one or two boys become angry. They reacted by hitting books or the table.

A faculty member ran in and his first words were, "There is now going to be the largest manhunt in the history of this country!"

Most of the people that I saw simply sat there in complete shock and distress. They didn't know how to react.

Whether people around us were democrats or republicans made no difference. Our realization was that our country's president had been shot.

While listening to the thunderous volume of the radio in this library, which was usually a dominion of perfect silence, I walked over to the large window which overlooked the entire campus from that vantage point in the Social-Religious Building.

Very few students were out walking on the campus, but I looked and saw a young man frantically running toward the flagpole which was situated in a corner spot on campus between the West Dormitory and the Social-Religious Building.

I did not know the name of this student, but I had seen him on campus many times. He suffered from cerebral palsy, and it was an effort for him to walk, especially if he wanted to walk fast.

I stood at the window and watched this young man as he moved quickly, fighting to move his body, while wearing a distressed look on his face.

It took him several minutes, but at a speed as fast as his body could manage, he reached the flagpole on campus. He quickly lowered the flag to half-staff. After his mission had been completed, he turned with his head down and slowly moved away from the flagpole in his usual manner of strenuous walking.

Where were you on November 22, 1963? I imagine you saw a great diversity of reactions from the people around you.

As for me, this shocking event promulgated many reactions from people that I saw. Some were angry, some cried, some were frustrated, many were in shock, some were distressed, all felt sorrow, and I even saw one person react by making his way to the flagpole to lower the American flag to half-staff.

Thanksgiving

Thanksgiving Through the Years

I have always looked upon Thanksgiving Day as a religious holiday. Thanksgiving is a day set aside each year for giving thanks to God for blessings received during the year. The elements of celebration are family reunions, feasting, prayer, and praise.

As a child I can remember sitting down to a wonderful Thanksgiving dinner that my mother prepared. We had our usual blessing before the meal. Sometimes, before we had the blessing, I remember that each of us around the table spoke one at a time revealing what wonderful thing we were thankful for in our lives. I can remember even today some of those things which each of us was thankful.

The first Thanksgiving Days in New England were harvest festivals. They were days for thanking God for the farmers' plentiful crops. For this reason, the holiday still takes place late in the Fall after the crops have been gathered.

History tells us that the first Thanksgiving in New England was celebrated in Plymouth less than a year after the Plymouth colonists had settled in America. The first dreadful winter in Massachusetts had killed about half of the members of the colony.

But, new hope arose in the Summer of 1621. History reveals that the settlers expected a good corn harvest, despite poor crops of peas, wheat, and barley. Thus, in early Autumn, Governor William Bradford arranged a harvest festival to give thanks to God for the progress the colony had made.

The festival lasted three days. The men of Plymouth, being good hunters, shot ducks, geese, and turkeys. The women cooked over outdoor fires to prepare the feast. The festival friends enjoyed a menu of fish, wild plums, corn bread, and watercress, in addition to the ducks, geese, and turkeys.

About ninety American-Indians also attended the festival. They brought five deer to add to the feast.

After the American Revolution, the first national Thanksgiving Day proclaimed by President George Washington was November 26, 1789. It was to be a day of national Thanksgiving.

Later, President Abraham Lincoln proclaimed the last Thursday in November of 1863 as "a day of Thanksgiving and praise to our beneficent Father."

Each year afterward, for seventy-five years, the presidents formally proclaimed that Thanksgiving Day should be celebrated on the last Thursday of November.

But, many of us remember that in the years 1939, 1940, and 1941, President Franklin D. Roosevelt set Thanksgiving Day one week earlier for economic reasons. He wanted to help businesses by lengthening the shopping time prior to Christmas. You will remember that some critics of the president enjoyed referring to the day as Franksgiving Day!

At any rate, Congress ruled that after 1941, Thanksgiving Day would return to the fourth Thursday of November, and it would be a legal federal holiday.

A Happy Thanksgiving to everyone, and let us always remember to stress the THANKS and the GIVING in our Thanksgiving Day.

Christmas

A Nostalgic Christmas

Before moving to Bellevue, our family lived in West Meade Hills on Pennywell Drive. We raised our two children there on the steep hill which we affectionately called Pennywell Mountain.

Some winters were pretty rough. If the ice and snow came, we had to leave our cars at the bottom of our steep driveway. If we had gotten groceries, we had to lug the bags up steep Pennywell Mountain.

However, it was nice to look out back from our house on up the mountain and see a beautiful blanket of snow, and some spectacular visions of ice trimmed tree branches. It was not uncommon to see several deer slowly moving about. We enjoyed a large variety of colorful birds coming up to our bird feeders in search of food.

A few days before Christmas one year, I remember sitting by my dear wife before a crackling fire in our den fireplace. Both of us seemed to have a lot to talk about, and a lot of memories to capture.

We watched the snowflakes drift down outside the window. We delighted in the smell of hickory wood burning in the fireplace. My mind also delighted in drifting back to beautiful memories of days gone by.

I remembered Christmas when I was a child. My mother made hot biscuits from scratch every morning, and for Christmas Day she baked a chocolate cake and a coconut cake. It was a tradition.

In addition, each Christmas my grandmother gave my father and his brother a most fantastic fruit cake which she made from scratch. She always baked a large, light fruit cake and a large, dark fruit cake of equal size. Then, for Christmas she cut them in half and gave a full fruit cake of half light and half dark to my father and his family, and one to his brother and his family.

We always trimmed a tree with a few ornaments. We received a few gifts, and we gave a few gifts at Christmas time. My sister and I each Christmas morning left the house into the fresh, crisp, wintry air carrying a basket with some small gifts to give to our friends, and to see what each of them had received for Christmas. My mother always had several small gift "spares" wrapped in case we ran into someone to whom we needed to give a gift.

We enjoyed attending the Christmas Eve service at church. We tried to visit some older friends to lift their spirits on Christmas Day. We had our traditions.

My wife enjoyed reflecting on her memories, too. When she was a child, Christmas Eve church service was important. On Christmas Day each year, many members of her family met at her Aunt Ruth's and Uncle Walter's home. Her Uncle Newtie always dressed in a Santa Claus suit and gave out the presents from under the tree. My wife's grandfather presented each child there with a brand new, shiny half-dollar. It was a treasure.

Now, our children and grandchildren are forming their traditions for them to reflect on in later years. What a pleasure it is for my wife and me to be a part of their lives and traditions now.

May each celebration of the season be a happy one for all, and one in which all of us can reflect on God's richest blessings.

HAPPY HOLIDAYS TO ALL!

Times, People, Places and Things

A variety of memories--
A smorgasbord of Nashville's nostalgic tastes

National Life & Accident Insurance Co. with WSM radio on top floor. YMHA building is on the left.

Times, People, Places and Things

Here is a variety of memories--a smorgasbord of Nashville's nostalgic tastes--I am fixin' to dish up for you.

I was born and grew up in Nashville during The Great Depression of the 1920s and 1930s. Somehow our minds seem to filter out all of the hard times, disappointments, and miserable moments of the past, and we are blessed with remembering mainly the good and happy times which we experienced and which still bring happiness to our lives. Remembering with a nostalgic spirit makes us happy.

While driving down Woodmont Boulevard the other day, I remembered that this street used to be made of concrete from Hillsboro Road to Harding Road. In fact, we called the street Concrete Boulevard.

My thoughts began to reflect on how many times, people, places and things in Nashville used to be something different.

I remember when the educational television station (WDCN-TV) was on channel 2, and then the station switched with WSIX-TV and went to channel 8. Today, the educational or public television station has the call letters WNPT-TV, and old WSIX-TV is now WKRN-TV.

I remember the restaurant at the edge of Centennial Park across the street from the old Hippodrome and the present Holiday Inn Select Vanderbilt. I remember when the location was glorified by a great Italian restaurant called Punaro's. It was owned by James Punaro who was a violinist in the Nashville Symphony Orchestra. Many times, the restaurant would be full of guests, and Jimmy would take out his violin and sit right in the middle of the tables and begin to play. What a wonderful experience!

After changing hands, the restaurant became the Natchez Trace Restaurant. It served one of the finest and most inexpensive steaks in town. Now, that location is occupied by a McDonald's and its parking lot.

Speaking of restaurants, do you remember the great food served on Sixth Avenue, North downtown? We had the B & W Cafeteria, Cross Keyes, and Kleeman's restaurants. You must remember Kleeman's for their terrific recipe for apple pie. After Kleeman's departed, that great apple pie recipe went to the Downstairs Dinette at Harvey's department store. Even Harvey's is gone now.

Back in those days, a great date would be to go downtown, have a nice dinner, then go to a movie at the Paramount, Loew's or Knickerbocker theatre, and then have a great dessert at Candyland at the corner of Seventh and Church.

To make some money or receive prizes, did you ever sell magazines such as *Saturday Evening Post, Collier's, Ladies' Home Journal, Grit,* or *Woman's Home Companion*? I went from door to door selling to our neighbors. I usually knew who would buy and who wouldn't.

I remember the old Lebeck Brothers department store on Church Street. The elevator there was just a metal cage, and was wide open as it slowly went up to the second floor.

If you did any shopping downtown in the old days, you remember stores such as Grimes and Gilbert's which utilized wire baskets that carried what you bought on overhead wires to the office to be sacked. Also, your payment at some stores was shot up to the office in leather tubes.

I remember Burk's on Church Street between Fourth and Fifth Avenues. I used to get my photographic equipment and supplies there. The Sun Trust Bank occupies that area now.

When I was a child, I can remember my family eating lunch at Shacklett's Cafeteria, and then walking across Church Street to Burk's where they had a free weighing scales outside the door. (Come to think of it, that was a pretty stupid time to weigh just after we had eaten!)

The Belmont Theatre was at the corner of Blakemore Avenue and 21st Avenue, South. The theatre entrance was right on the corner.

The last time I was in the Belmont Theatre was in the early 1940s when our English teacher, Miss Austin at West End High School, took our last period English class there to see *The House of the Seven Gables* by Nathaniel Hawthorne. That was good literature, a fine teaching device, and great fun.

The old Governor's mansion was located at 2118 West End Avenue. I remember when it was torn down and a fast food restaurant was built at that location. Now, even the fast food restaurant is gone.

Can you remember when there was no such thing as a fast food restaurant in Nashville? Those were the old, old days when I am sure we were more nutritionally healthy!

———————

Downtown there was a Peach's Drugstore which had a wonderful lunchroom called Peach's. The owner's daughter married a man with whom I worked for a while at Griffin art and office supply company.

Hettie Ray's was first a restaurant downtown. Later, Hettie Ray's was a dinner club on top of Nine Mile Hill as US Highway 70 went toward Bellevue from Nashville. (Nine Mile Hill meaning nine miles from Nashville. When the horse and mule-drawn wagons came in from the West, the drivers knew that they were nine miles from Nashville when they got to that hill.)

Many of the school sororities and fraternities held their dinner-dances at Hettie Ray's. Later, it became the Biltmore Dinner Club. Wessex Towers condominiums stand atop that spot today.

I played the Biltmore once. I can remember driving out the old, two-lane Highway 70 with another saxophone player at Peabody by the name of Jody Holt. After the job, I can remember that we went back out toward the Peabody campus, and stopped at a Toddle House to get something to eat. The old Toddle House restaurants served those hash-brown potatoes. Of course, we can still get something similar at the Waffle House restaurants. Do you remember that the old Toddle House restaurants had you pay your bill by dropping your money in a container as you went out the door?

I remember the organ concerts by Leon Cole at Centennial Park's old band shell. The old band shell was at the same location as the present stage in the park. I played in bands at both of them many times.

Mary Elizabeth Hicks played organ at WLAC radio, but also she could be seen playing the organ as it rose from the pit to the stage level at the Paramount Theatre. Other organists played there, for instance Leon Cole. Later, Bob Luck was the organist at the Paramount.

Back in the old days, we called eye glasses spectacles. Hose we called stockings. Suspenders were called galluses. Topcoats back then were called overcoats. Men's underwear was called BVDs, and ladies' underwear was called teddies.

Do you remember Skeets Mayo, an old vaudeville man, who owned a costume shop downtown?

Do you remember when the Shelby Street Bridge over the Cumberland River was known as the Sparkman Street Bridge? Do you remember Sidebottom's Ice Cream? Do you remember the home located on West End Avenue which had the name "Old Ladies Home?" It was torn down several years ago.

Did you ever go see wrestling at the old Hippodrome? It was located where the Holiday Inn Select Vanderbilt sits today. Nick Gulas was the entrepreneur who promoted the wrestling matches. If you attended, then you remember the Welsh Brothers, Farmer Brown, Len Rossi, Tojo Yamamoto, Jackie Fargo, and others. I was there in the 1950s the night that Gorgeous George wrestled. Television had made him and others very popular stars.

Also, if you attended the wrestling matches, you remember War Horse Rogers. He sat ringside and rang the gong for each match. He would ring the gong only three times. People would scream and try to make him ring it a fourth time. Sometimes he would smile and play like he was going to ring the gong again after three times. But, he never did.

You might remember when Hank Fort wrote "I Didn't Know the Gun Was Loaded." It was a very popular song at the time. Everybody sang it.

We remember the fireside chats by President Franklin Delano Roosevelt.

Not many of us remember when the water reservoir on Eighth Avenue South ruptured in 1912. I was not around. My mother and father were dating back then. They told me that they, along with my mother's sister and her boy friend, went over to Eighth Avenue when they heard about the disaster. They said that the reservoir split from top to bottom and sent twenty-five million gallons of water rushing down the hill flooding hundreds of people out of their homes.

Do you remember when Carl Hinkle, Baby Ray, Gene Hosse, and Bill Wade played football for Vanderbilt? Do you remember when Red Sanders was the football coach at Vandy before he went to coach at UCLA?

Do you remember the names Dan McGugin and Ray Morrison who coached football at Vanderbilt? Jess Neely coached football at Rhodes College (back then it was Southwestern), Rice University, University of Alabama, and Clemson College. Jess was Vandy's athletic director for a time.

We used to be able to go up into the tower of the State Capitol Building. Now, the old metal staircase is chained off.

Dr. Alfred Leland Crabb taught at George Peabody College and wrote several historical novels capturing a romantic image of our early Nashville. He wrote *Breakfast at the Hermitage*, *Dinner at Belmont*, *Supper at the Maxwell House*, among others.

In 1947, I was privileged to be in Dr. Crabb's English class titled "Writing for Publication" during the time he was doing his writing.

The first book I read by Dr. Crabb was *Lodging at the Saint Cloud*. The Saint Cloud House was a hotel downtown at the corner of Fifth Avenue and Church Street during the days of the Civil War. The hotel was located diagonally across the street from the present Downtown Presbyterian Church building which still stands. During the Civil War after Nashville had been captured, both the church and the hotel were occupied by the Union troops. The church was used as a hospital.

The *Grand Ole Opry* started as the "WSM Barn Dance" by George D. Hay in 1925. A couple of years later, the Solemn Old Judge was ready to come on the air following Dr. Walter Damrosch's NBC program called *Music Appreciation Hour*. Judge Hay said something like, "For the past hour, we have been listening to music taken largely from Grand Opera. Now, we will present the *Grand Ole Opry*." The name stuck.

Can you remember the dance studio of Eva Thompson Jones? It was in an upstair space on Church Street between Fourth and Fifth Avenues across from Burk's Company. It was her uncle, Jimmy Thompson, who was a performer right at the beginning of the old WSM Barn Dance to become the *Grand Ole Opry*. His niece, who accompanied him at the piano was Eva Thompson Jones.

You are a real old-timer if you can remember back to the 1940s when Francis Craig and His Orchestra did a Sunday afternoon show at the War Memorial Auditorium with a singer at WSM at the time by the name of Jeri Southern. The announcer for those shows was WSM's Jud Collins.

———

Do you remember some commercials we used to hear such as the one by Harold L. Shyer? He would say, "If you don't know diamonds, then know your jeweler. And, if Harold says it's so, it's so."

Speaking of jewelers, do you remember Brodnax Jewelers? They offered fine jewelry to Nashville since 1897.

Do you remember Marshall Whitley Jewelers? Back in his old high school days, Marshall was the drum major for the East High Marching Band. Also, Marshall was the drum major for the Post 5 American Legion Band back in the 40s, 50s, and beyond when the band marched in parades and went on Legion state and national conventions.

Fred Waller and John Coles owned Coles and Waller Jewelers on Union Street. I bought my wife's engagement ring from Fred more than fifty years ago.

Fred Waller also was a wonderful tenor soloist. He sang at WSM radio and Hobson Methodist Church as well as many places around town. After Fred's wife had been dead for some time, he married Mary Elizabeth Hicks who had been a pianist and organist at radio stations WLAC, WSM, and WSIX.

Fred Waller passed away several years ago, and Mary Liz still lives in Nashville. Their music brought real quality to Music City USA.

———————

Were you around in 1937? I was thirteen years old. If you were in Nashville, then you remember the Cumberland River flooding. For an example, the area that is now the James Robertson Parkway below the State Capitol building was under water.

Also, at other times, the Cumberland River froze over so hard that we could walk on it. I guess it froze over many times over years gone by. But, I remember January 1940 when a neighbor on our street took several of us kids down to First Avenue and Broad Street. We parked the car and walked out on the ice which covered the usual, rapidly flowing river.

I remember the old Saint Thomas Hospital when it was close to downtown between Church and Hayes Streets. Of course, many years ago Saint Thomas moved to new facilities off of Harding Road where it is located today.

The old Protestant Hospital was across Church Street from the old Saint Thomas Hospital. The Protestant Hospital was an old, red brick building sitting back off of Church Street. Inside the hospital, I remember a beautiful marble stairway. The old Protestant Hospital later became the Baptist Hospital at that location. Over the years, Baptist has added many buildings to the giant complex as we know it today.

I remember when Roy Acuff was a candidate for Governor of Tennessee back in 1948, and Tex Ritter ran for the U. S. Senate from Tennessee in 1970. Who knows! It may have been very interesting for Tennessee if they had won!

While sitting here eating some Girl Scout cookies which we purchased from one of our granddaughters, I remember that it was 1975 when nine-year-old Marsha Trimble was murdered. Marsha disappeared while delivering some Girl Scout cookies in her neighborhood. The rape and murder have not been solved up to this time.

———◆———

There were some great old hotels which are no longer with us. Several were of special interest to me. Gone is the old, glorious Maxwell House Hotel with all of its history. Gone is the Andrew Jackson Hotel where the DeeJay conventions used to gather. The hotel was noted for hiring live bands over many years.

I remember a night that I was playing a nice dinner-dance in the ballroom of the Andrew Jackson, and Fred Waring and His Pennsylvanians were playing a concert over in the War Memorial Auditorium. His entire group was staying at the Andrew Jackson Hotel. When the Waring concert was over, some of his players came over and sat-in with the band in which I was playing. They were some wonderful players, too.

The Andrew Jackson stood next to the old Elks Club on Sixth Avenue, North. Both the hotel and the Elks Club building were torn down to make room for our present state building and Tennessee Performing Arts Center.

Gone is the Tulane Hotel at Eighth Avenue and Church Street downtown where some of Nashville's first recordings were made. Castle Recording Company was located there.

The Noel Hotel building is still downtown at the corner of Fourth Avenue, North, but it is not the Noel Hotel where you can have a good meal and hold dinner-dances. At one time, WLAC radio had a breakfast club type broadcast in the mornings from the ballroom of the Noel Hotel. The old Noel Hotel building is now the Prudential Securities Building.

Matt's Newstand and the Palace Hatters were located on Fourth Avenue down from the Noel Hotel.

———————

I hope you remember some past, fine music stores in Nashville, such as Strobel's Music Shop in the Arcade, French Music Company, Roy Warden Piano Company, L. C. Tiller, John G. Miller Instrument Company, Jack Kendall's Nashville Band Instrument Company, Claude P. Street Piano Company which is still with us, and Hewgley's Music Shop which is not with us now.

Do you remember hearing the voice of Larry Munson as he broadcast the Nashville Vols baseball games? WLAC's Herman Grizzard was the public address announcer at Sulphur Dell ballpark, Ken Berryhill announced on the old WMAK radio station when it was located on the ground floor of the old Maxwell House Hotel, Ken Bramming played good music on WSM-FM, and David Cobb played great classical music programs on WSM-AM radio way back in time.

We had the great sports columns in the newspapers by Grantland Rice, John Bibb, and Fred Russell, all deceased. Fred was the last to pass away in January of 2003.

Did you ever know the likeable and entertaining Jimmy Sanders? He owned the Sanders Manufacturing Company which produced novelties of every description.

Jimmy was a very good magician. Once, the band in which I was playing went out to the old Clover Bottom Home to take some entertainment and a little happiness to the residents' lives. Jimmy Sanders went with the band. He did some magic tricks that actually entertained me. He was very funny and a very generous man in lending help to other Nashvillians.

I remember when McClure's was located in Hillsboro Village on 21st Avenue, South. I went to their close-out sale many years ago before the store moved to Highway 100 near the Highway 70 split. Then, as of 2002, McClure's was no more.

Have you ever noticed the two stone columns from a gateway standing across Harding Road in front of The Temple and the Belle Meade Plantation? The two stone columns stand between Harding Road and the railroad tracks. Years ago, those columns formed the gateway to Nashville's Gun Club. Back within the residential area today, there is a street called Gun Club Road.

Did you ever go to Dunbar Cave or Ruskin Cave? Do you remember going to Red Boiling Springs where people enjoyed various mineral waters and good Southern cooking which defies adequate words of description?

Did you ever sleep on a feather bed? As a child, I slept on a feather bed when my family visited our relatives who lived on a farm at Cherry Valley near Watertown, Tennessee. The feather bed was right beside the chifforobe not far from the pitcher of well-water sitting beside the wash pan.

———

I remember Nashvillian Tom Tichenor who performed with his marionettes and puppets. Tom was featured on a childrens' show on channel 4 television in the afternoons back in the 1950s. I had the pleasure of writing, performing and directing the music on one of those old shows. Also, my wife directed elementary school kids playing tonettes on that show. Marjorie Cooney, who was at WSM radio for many years and later at WSM-TV, produced the television show. That is when WSM-TV studios and their first tower were located on a hill behind Belmont University above Compton and Bernard Avenues.

Poindexter, the hound dog, was on those shows with Tom. I remember that when I talked to Poindexter on that show, Tom had to keep reminding me, "When you talk to Poindexter, don't look at my mouth. Look at Poindexter's mouth!"

Tom Tichenor was a long-standing feature of happiness for children in Nashville. He and his puppets and marionettes performed regular children shows at the Nashville Public Library. Also, Tom opened his home on Thompson Lane every Christmas season for visitors to enjoy his attractive decorations and his display of puppets, marionettes, and costumes.

Tom was away from Nashville for a while performing in New York City when he was the featured puppeteer in the Broadway musical *Carnival*.

———

Bill Barry and Bill Baird once owned radio station WFMB, 105.9 on the FM dial. At that time, it was the only FM radio station in Nashville.

That station did remotes of events around town. I remember playing in Bob Hamp's Orchestra out on the terrace at the Colemere Country Club in the summer of 1963 when Bill Baird was the announcer for an hour remote broadcast of the band playing for the Saturday night dinner-dance.

Also, that station did a remote from the Municipal Auditorium for Governor Buford Ellington's inauguration. Ernie Keller, whom you may remember from old WSM radio, served as the master-of-ceremonies.

Bill Barry and Bill Baird later sold WFMB-FM which today is WLAC-FM.

———••◦••———

I remember how fabric stores used to sell cloth to ladies for use in sewing. I can remember when my mother would buy three yards of cloth at a dry goods store. The saleslady would take a bolt of cloth, unravel some of the cloth, stretch out the cloth from the tip of her nose to the tips of her fingers three times. Then, she would add just a little bit more, and cut the cloth off at that point. That was considered three yards of cloth. I wish things were as simple as that today!

At one time, Fifth Avenue downtown was the center of our shopping. We had the five-and-ten-cent stores, Woolworth, Kress, Grants, and McLellan's. I remember how these stores sold sheet music.

There was a square area of shelves or counters with sheet music displayed all around the square. A piano was sitting in the center. If a customer wanted to hear a certain piece of sheet music, the saleslady would sit down at the piano and play the song.

If you lived around Blair Boulevard and 21st Avenue South, you probably remember the Blankenship Drugstore on the corner. After the drugstore was gone and more than thirty years later, you could still see written on the building on the Blair Boulevard side, the words: "Blankenship Drugs, Enoch E. Hartman, Jr., Pharmacist."

Following Blankenship's stay, Compton's Foodland took over that area where the grocery store stayed for 30 years. However, on Saturday, July 15, 2000, Compton's sold its last groceries at that location and closed its doors. There is still a Compton's Foodland at 2900 West End Avenue.

During the year 2001, that building at 21st and Blair burned to the ground. Soon after, work began on a new Harris Teeter Grocery Store which sits at that location today.

Between Ashwood Avenue and Blair Boulevard on 21st Avenue, South, there was a fish pond out in front of the fire hall. That pond was something that all of the children loved. The fish pond is gone, but the fire hall is still there.

You will have to be a real Nashville old-timer to remember the permanent amusement rides which were at the fairgrounds. A wooden roller coaster which was called "The Big Dipper" was a permanent fixture at the Fairgrounds. Also, on the hill leading up to the automobile tunnel and the grandstand, we could ride the "Whip" and the "Old Mill."

On the other side of the street was all of the children's favorite carousel which we simply called the "Merry-Go-Round." When I was a real small child, my father would ride the Merry-Go-Round with me, and he was able to reach up and grab what they called "the gold ring" as the ride passed. With this gold ring, you were allowed to have another ride free.

Then, in 1951, Fair Park came into existence at the site where you entered the Fairgrounds from Wedgewood Avenue. That park had a ghost ride which went by the name "Paris After Dark," a "Ferris Wheel," a track with little autos that you could drive called "The Turnpike," a shooting gallery, a ride called "Tilt-a-Whirl," and a train ride on tracks which circled the park, as well as other things. Also, the name of the old "Big Dipper" roller coaster was changed to "Skyliner."

In 1985, Fair Park was used in scenes for the movie *Sweet Dreams* starring Jessica Lang. The movie was about the life of Patsy Cline. That movie was one of about five in which our son, Jeff, acted as an extra. Fair Park is no longer!

———

Did you ever go to old Jefferson Springs down on Stones River? When I was a child, we referred to the spot simply as "Old Jefferson."

During The Great Depression, families had to think up things to do which would not require a lot of money. My family enjoyed going to Old Jefferson for swimming. Each time we went, my mother packed a good picnic lunch for us to eat out in the great surroundings of Mother Nature.

The water of the Stones River was wonderful. I remember that the big kids had a rope hanging out over the river with which they could take a running jump and drop into the water.

I was about five and my sister was about twelve. We had some fun too. As soon as we got to Old Jefferson, our daddy would jack up the old car, and take the innertubes out of the tires so my sister and I could sit in them out on the water.

When we finished our swimming, picnic, and family outing, Daddy would put the innertubes back in the tires and back on the car. Nothing was too much trouble for our mother and daddy to do for us to have a good, wholesome and enjoyable time.

We would head for home with wonderful memories, and a great deal of happiness even during The Great Depression.

———⋙◆⋘———

The Iris Room was at the Cain-Sloan Company downtown. Also, I can't think of Cain-Sloan without thinking about Bunnyland which the store staged each Easter season. My sister took our two children to Bunnyland every year. It was an Easter tradition.

Do you remember those small Dixie Cups at drinking fountains? You would pull a Dixie Cup from the holder by the water tank, get a good, cold cup of water, and watch the bubbles come up in the big water bottle. Actually, those water tanks are coming back. My daughter, Lee Anne, had one in her home.

If you ever rode on passenger trains, you remember walking to the front of the coach as it swayed back and forth to the rhythmic rolling motion over the tracks, and you would take out a Dixie Cup for a drink of water. Then, when you tried to throw away the used cup, due to the movement of the train, you would miss the bucket.

Kids on the train would get a cup of water about 15 times during the trip!

Speaking of when I was a kid, how many of you remember some good and old comic strips in the "funny paper" such as Gasoline Alley, Bringing Up Father, Katzenjammer Kids, Moon Mullins, Toonerville Folks, Tillie the Toiler, Li'l Abner, and Jane Arden?

We used to enjoy the old drive-in theatres. We had the Crescent, Bel-Aire, Bordeaux, Warner Park, Montague, Skyway, Colonial, Donelson, and Sunset to name a few. A big thanks to the Broadway Drive-in located between White Bluff and Dickson, Tennessee on U. S. Highway 70. It is still in operation today after more than half a century.

Do you remember Kusan, Inc., the Nashville-based manufacturer? That company received the Symbol of Excellence award by officials of Sears-Roebuck back in 1976.

How many of you remember when Sears-Roebuck was located downtown at Eighth and Church? It was next to the Paramount Theatre, and across the street from where the Tulane Hotel stood.

A tall SEARS sign was on the Eighth Avenue side of the Sears building just like the tall PARAMOUNT sign was in front of the theatre on Church Street.

That corner location at Eighth and Church is now occupied by the Tennessee Department of Health and Environment Bureau of Medicaid.

Do you ever long for one of those great frosty malts that we used to get at Cato's fountain and restaurant in the Arcade?

Do you remember the old Coca-Cola sign that told the time of day which sat up high at the intersection of West End Avenue and Broadway?

———

The Episcopal church which sits at the corner of Ninth Avenue, North and Broadway downtown was the first Episcopal Church in Nashville. It was organized at the Masonic Hall in 1829. The same tower bell is still at the church which rang for the second inauguration of President Andrew Jackson, and the inauguration of President James K. Polk.

The original name of the church was Christ Church. You can see that on the cornerstone while standing on the sidewalk on Broadway in front of the church. Later, the name became Christ Episcopal Church to identify it from other churches with a similar name.

Today, the accurate name of the church is Christ Church Cathedral because, in addition to serving a parish, now the church also serves as the seat of the Bishop of Tennessee. I had the opportunity to perform in that beautiful church back when I was playing in the Nashville Symphony Orchestra.

———

Sometimes it is hard for tourists to find their way around Nashville. Streets change names too much for them. For instance, downtown Broadway heading west becomes West End Avenue, then it becomes Harding Road, and all the time it is also U. S. Highway 70.

Robertson Road becomes White Bridge Road, then becomes Woodmont Boulevard, and then becomes Thompson Lane. I am sure you can think of at least two dozen more examples.

Do you recall Nashvillians referring to Union street as "The Wall Street of the South?"

———————

Did you ever eat at the establishment called The Terminal Lunch which sat between the rear of the old Main Post Office and Union Station? Do you remember old Applegate's Landing on Nolensville Road? That restaurant had its salad bar on an old 1931 Model-A Ford pick-up truck.

I am sure you remember the Flaming Steer restaurant which was located for many years at 19th and West End Avenues. You could get good and inexpensive steaks there. Today, a Mrs. Winner's is located on that corner.

The Hearth was a restaurant located at 701 Gallatin Road which used the advertising phrase, "An evening of remarkable dining in the French tradition."

Shakey's was the former pizza place on Richard Jones Road off Hillsboro Road in Green Hills. Shakey's entertained its customers with live Dixieland music and silent movies.

We had the Sailmaker restaurant where we could have seen Little Bo Peep, Superman, and other servers in costume. Agner's Market and Restaurant was at Eighth and Broad. In there you could eat lunch, and then do some grocery shopping.

The Satsuma is still downtown on Union Street, and the restaurant began serving back in 1918. Can you remember when Kinnard's restaurant was located at 21st Avenue, South and Blair Boulevard?

Today, we have many wonderful restaurants in Nashville, but the closing of one of the old ones will be hard for me to forget. I loved the spaghetti we used to get at Marchetti's located on 19th Avenue just south of West End Avenue. Today, another good restaurant, the Midtown Café, occupies that location.

——————

Another good time to remember was when we had a boat on the Cumberland River named the Idlewild. Of course, we have some nice boats there now.

Do you remember when the Golden Gloves was a top topic on the sports pages of newspapers all over the country?

In the old days, when most all of our shopping was done downtown, Gilbert's sold boys' wear, and Lebeck Brothers, Tinsley's, and Loveman's sold women's and girls' wear. Charles P. Ellis Company, Petway-Reavis and others sold men's wear.

I remember Nashville's minor league ice hockey team called the Dixie Flyers. They played their games at the new Municipal Auditorium. In 1966, the Dixie Flyers played through the playoffs, winning all eleven of their games, to win their first league title and Walker Cup.

The name reminds me of the old Dixie Flyer passenger train which my family rode so many times in the 1930s when I was a child. We rode it between Nashville and Chattanooga. Our neighbor two doors down from our house was Mr. Jim Kilgore who was a conductor on the Dixie Flyer. I looked up to him as a celebrity. The old Franklin Interurban ran from Nashville to Franklin on tracks parallel to Franklin Pike some of the way. It was like a commuter train, but it was really a streetcar powered by electricity.

———

There used to be an historic building downtown located on Eighth Avenue, South near Demonbreun Street. It was built in 1914 and had carried the names of Women's Club and the Centennial Club. This old Centennial Club built in a Spanish-mission style of architecture was where a women's activist group during World War II rolled bandages and sent them to soldiers overseas.

The building was sold to the Union Rescue Mission, and then they sold it to the First Baptist Church. The old building burned in December of 2000. The building remains were torn down, and the area now is a parking lot.

That old building holds some memories for me. When I was twelve years old, I began taking accordion lessons at Claude P. Street Piano Company when the store was located on Church Street next to and across the alley from the Paramount Theatre.

One year the teachers held a big recital in the Centennial Club building with all of the accordion students. All of the students played in a large accordion band as well as some students playing solos. I recall that the solo I played that night was "The Blue Danube Waltz" by Strauss.

The new Centennial Club is located on Abbott Martin Road in Green Hills.

———◆———

People all over the country used to shop at a company called Montgomery Ward. When I was a child, Nashville had a large Montgomery Ward store. I remember one year when the store offered free tap dancing lessons to kids. My sister, Elva, and some neighbors took some lessons.

As of the year 2001, sorrowfully, Montgomery Ward went out of business after a run of 125 years.

———◆———

If you were ever an automobile enthusiast, then you remember the DeSoto coupe, Pontiac sedan, Hudson, Edsel, Studebaker, Chevrolet Fleetline, Kaiser, Frazier, Willis, Datsun, Packard, the Buick Super Sedan, Marathon, and Dusenburg.

Back in the early 1950s, I was one of those who just had to have a Nash. You probably remember. Nash came out with a model which looked like an up-side-down bathtub. Yeah, I had one of those!

In 1999, I bought a new Plymouth. Then, I learned that the Chrysler Corporation was doing away with the Plymouth brand line.

Then, we watched the work crew take down the Hippodrome Olds sign of the auto dealer on Broadway because General Motors announced that they were going to discontinue the Oldsmobile brand line. So, the old neon sign came down which had been a fixture on Broadway since the early 1950s.

The neon sign displayed over the dealership first began advertising "Hippodrome Ford" in the 1950s. Then, the sign was changed to "Hippodrome Olds" around 1964.

Well, maybe my grandchildren can write about the Plymouth and the Oldsmobile like I now write about the DeSoto and the Nash!

———

Do you remember back to the days when we were kids, and the worst language we heard were expressions like Gee-Whiz, often spoken by radio's Henry Aldrich when he got into trouble?

We might have heard such expressions as Doggone It, Dad Blame It, Golly Gee, and once in a while a shocking expression like Gol Darned! I am sure you can remember Great Guns, I Declare, Good Granny, My Stars, and To Heck With It.

———

Before we had Interstates, we enjoyed looking over the countryside as we drove on old two-lane roads. Along the road, we could enjoy reading the Burma Shave advertisement signs. There were five signs posted about 100 feet apart, each containing one line of a 4-line quatrain poem or limerick. Of course, the fifth sign always advertised Burma Shave.

You might have seen:

Don't lose your head... To gain a minute... You need your head... Your brains are in it... BURMA SHAVE.

Don't put your arm... Out the window too far... Or it'll ride home... In another car... BURMA SHAVE!

You can do... A mile a minute... But there ain't... No future in it... BURMA SHAVE!

Somebody stop me! !

Passing cars... When you can't see... May get you a glimpse... Of eternity... BURMA SHAVE!

The one who drives... When he's been drinking... Depends on you... To do his thinking... BURMA SHAVE!

Please! Just one more!

Brother Speeders... Let's rehearse... All together... Good morning nurse... BURMA SHAVE!

I hope this smorgasbord of Times, People, Places and Things brings some nice nostalgic tastes and memories back to you with a relish of happiness.

We could sit and cry about "the good old days," but instead, we need to look to the future for even greater things to come.

Index of Names

A

Acklen, Adelicia 14, 33
Acklen, Joseph 14, 33
Acuff, Roy 157, 249
Acuff, Roy Jr. 157
Aldrich, Henry 263
Allen, Bill "Hoss" 106-108
Alley, Elmer 148
Alley, Pete 131
Ammonette, Bill 126-127
Ammonette, Marge 126
Anderson, Marian 22
Austin, Miss (teacher) 242

B

Bailey, Cecil 145
Bailey, John E. 97
Baird, Bill 166-167, 253
Barnet, Charlie 39
Barrows, Cliff 161
Barry, Bill 165-167, 253
Barrymore, Ethel 21
Bart, Teddy 108
Bass, Susanne Warner 87
Bate, Dr. Humphrey 148
Beasley, Alcyon Bate 148
Bell, Montgomery 26, 84,
    88, 169-172
Bell, Sam Davis 128
Benchley, Robert 101
Bennett, E. Lee 71
Benson, "Buzz" 167
Benton, Jesse (Mr. & Mrs.) 6
Benton, Thomas Hart 6
Berle, Milton 147
Berlin, Irving 208
Bernhardt, Sarah 21, 38
Berry, Colonel Harry S. 85
Berryhill, Ken xv, 250
Bess, Hattie "Tootsie" 106

Bess, Jeff 106
Bibb, John 251
Blackmer, Rip 6
Bloodworth, Kathy 110
Boguskie, Buster 3, 68
Bomar, Lynn 128
Bono, Sonny xvi
Boston, Ralph 164, 191
Bradford, Gov. William 234
Bradley, Owen 39, 125, 144
Brahms, Johannes 23
Bramming, Ken 167, 250
Brecia, Pete 144
Brentwood (vaudevillian) 99
Brewton, Dr. J. E. 27
Brittain, Bill 167
Brock, Senator Bill 128
Brown, Hillard 81
Browning, Gov. Gordon 28, 128
Bryan, William Jennings 38
Buchi, Sharon 177-178
Burgess, Smokey 68
Byrns, Joseph W. 128

C

Cantor, Eddie 146
Carroll, Gov. William 18
Carter, Dolly 176
Caruso, Enrico 22, 38
Cash, Johnny xvi, 23
Cassetty, Fred J. 131
Cavert, A. M. 97
Chance, "Lightning" 157
Chaplin, Charlie 21
Chaplin, James 197
Charry, Michael 139
Chayefsky Paddy 174
Cheek, Leslie 33-34
Cheek, Mrs. Leslie Wood 33-34
Cher xvi
Chester, Bob 147

G

Gaither, Bill   161
Gallagher, Jimmy   39
Gallo, Jack   167
Gant, Mr. (HV Farm)   83
Garfinkle, Elkin   128
Garland, Judy   123
Garrison, S. C.   27
Garvin, Clint   147
Gasser Brothers   183
Gatwood, Elden   142
Gibson, Don   157
Gilbert, Charlie   68
Gilbert, Larry   3, 67-68
Gillespie, Dizzy   163-164
Gilliam, Junior   191
Giuliani, Mayor Rudy   226
Goldsboro, Bobby   xvi
Goodrich, Andy   163
Gordy, "Papa" John   39
Gorgeous George (wrestler)   244
Gossage, Nancy   225
Graham, Rev. Billy   160-161
Gray, Glen   146
Greene, A. Roy   131
Griffin, Elva F.   v, 103, 170,
   227, 262
Griffin, Sara   96
Grizzard, Herman   105, 250
Groom, Syd   124
Grundy, Senator Felix   18, 26, 46
Guest, J. Hough   137
Gulas, Nick   2, 244
Gunter, Marcus   163
Gwinner, Haywood   174

H

Hadley, John   191
Hall, Cliff   214
Hall, Jon   125
Hampton, Lionel   164
Hardcastle, Walter   7-8, 44

Harding, John   32
Harding, Mary Elizabeth   33
Harding, Willie   45
Harding, William G.   32-33, 45
Harris, Jack   148
Harris, Phil   39, 124
Harrison, Rex   132
Hartman, Enoch E. Jr.   254
Harvey, Fred   133-134
Harvey, Fred Jr.   133-136
Hatcher, Joe   128
Hawkins, Coleman   163
Hawthorne, Nathaniel   242
Hay, George D.   246
Hayes, Helen   21
Heckman, Walter   124
Henkel, F. Arthur   137
Hepburn, Audrey   132
Hepburn, Katharine   21
Heriges, Robert M.   213
Hewgley, Tom   39
Hicks, Mary Eliz.   105, 107,
   244, 247-248
Higgins, Judge Bill   181
Hill, Albert E.   187
Hill, Dr. Henry H.   27
Hill, Horace G.   90
Hill, Horace G. Jr.   90
Hinkle, Carl   245
Holcomb, Joe   167
Holden, Fay   123
Holley, Horace   39, 203
Holt, J. D. "Jody"   243
Hope, Bob   22, 145
Horne, George   46
Hosse, Gene   245
Houdini, Harry   21
Howard, Gene   147
Howse, Hilary   128, 187
Hudson, Silvine   8
Hughes, Marvin   144
Hughes, Paul   82
Hull, Senator Cordell   15, 117
Hume, Alfred   8, 15, 17, 44
Hume, Rev. William   8, 44

Y

Yamamoto, Tojo   244
Yandle, Bill   39
Young, Adaline Moore   48
Young, Bob "Hamp"   39, 253
Young, T. C.   16, 18, 130, 186

Z

Zollicoffer, General Felix   18

Index of Businesses, Institutions, Places, and Things

PHOTO CREDITS

pp. xviii, 11, 31, 49, 92, 102, 189, 200 (North High School), 239, and book cover courtesy of Metropolitan Government Archives of Nashville and Davidson County.

p. vi photo by Jeff Thompson

p. 40 photo by Doug Underwood, 1961

p. 93 E.D.T. photo by Harvey's Cinefoto Studio, 1943

p. 206 photo by Bev LeCroy, 1972

pp. 10, 43, 53, 58, 61, 69, 93 (steam engine), 168, 179, 200 (University of Nashville) and 201, photos by E.D. Thompson

pp. 73, 129, 140, unknown

Printed in the United States
17083LVS00002B/20

9 780974 432236